HOW TO COMMUNICATE WITH SPIRITS

Open Yourself to the Possibilities

Arlene was a senior counselor at a high school. She had completed her records for the year, however the rest of the school was still in session, so she was required to be there. This presented her with some free time, so she began drawing some "caricatures." This activity was totally out of character for Arlene since she had no previous artistic ability whatsoever.

She felt she was being inspired. She started by drawing eyes, never knowing what the picture would become later. One picture in particular was an obvious rendering of a policeman, another a female belly dancer. The faces were exceptionally detailed.

After completing these drawings, Arlene led a workshop for the Human Development Center in Massachusetts. Twenty-seven people attended her workshop, and they were the exact same faces she had drawn previously, right down to a cop and a woman who was taking belly-dancing classes.

Arlene knew she was not actually drawing the pictures. Most of the drawings were signed by a spirit named David.

Has something similar happened to you?
Open yourself . . . .

About the Author

Elizabeth Owens is a certified medium and an ordained Spiritualist minister. She has appeared on such television shows as *The Other Side*, *CNN*, *Hard Copy*, and *Current Affair*. She teaches spiritual development classes in the Cassadaga Spiritualist Camp in Cassadaga, Florida, where she also lives. Elizabeth is also the author of *Women Celebrating Life* (Llewellyn).

To Write to the Author

If you wish to contact the author or would like more information about this book, please write to the author in care of Llewellyn Worldwide, and we will forward your request. Both the author and publisher appreciate hearing from you. Llewellyn Worldwide cannot guarantee that every letter written to the author can be answered, but all will be forwarded. Please write to:

Elizabeth Owens
℅ Llewellyn Worldwide
P.O. Box 64383, 1-56718-530-4
St. Paul, MN 55164-0383, U.S.A.

Please enclose a self-addressed, stamped envelope for reply, or $1.00 to cover costs. If outside the U.S.A., enclose international postal reply coupon.

Many of Llewellyn's authors have websites with additional information and resources. For more information, please visit our website at
http://www.llewellyn.com

HOW TO
COMMUNICATE
WITH SPIRITS

Elizabeth Owens

2002
Llewellyn Publications
St. Paul, Minnesota 55164-0383

FIRST EDITION
Second printing, 2002

Cover art: © Photodisc
Cover design: Gavin Dayton Duffy
Editing and book design: Christine Snow
Interior photos: Courtesy of Richard Bengtson, Edna Brobst, Bud Dickinson, Louis and Marie Gates, Anne Haughton, and Don Zanghi

Library of Congress Cataloging-in-Publication Data
Owens, Elizabeth, 1948–
    How to communicate with spirits / Elizabeth Owens.
        p. cm.
    Includes bibliographical references and index.
    ISBN 1-56718-530-4
    1. Spiritualism. I. Title.

BF1261.2.o94 2001
133.9–dc21   2001029826

APR 0 3 2002

Llewellyn Worldwide does not participate in, endorse, or have any authority or responsibility concerning private business transactions between our authors and the public.

All mail addressed to the author is forwarded but the publisher cannot, unless specifically instructed by the author, give out an address or phone number.

Any Internet references contained in this work are current at publication time, but the publisher cannot guarantee that a specific location will continue to be maintained. Please refer to the publisher's website for links to author websites and other sources.

Llewellyn Publications
A Division of Llewellyn Worldwide, Ltd.
P.O. Box 64383, Dept. 1-56718-530-4
St. Paul, MN 55164-0383
www.llewellyn.com

 Printed on recycled paper in the United States of America.

Acknowledgments

This book would not have been possible without the assistance of Fran Ellison. She fairly critiqued my words and ideas, while never failing to encourage me through the whole process of creating this book. Her knowledge of the subject and editing ability were paramount. My gratitude is impossible to convey effectively.

I am thankful to Nancy Mostad of Llewellyn Publications, for being so nice to work with and even sharing an experience about her spirit guides.

My everlasting gratitude to the following mediums and healers who shared their expertise and experiences with me: Rev. Patti Aubrey, Rev. Diane Davis, Rev. Sylvia DeLong, Fran Ellison, Rev. Jerry Frederich, Louis Gates, Marie Gates, Rev. Steven Hermann, Rev. Dr. Warren Hoover, Rev. Marie Lilla, Rev. Eloise Page, June Schmitt, Rev. Arlene Sikora, and Rev. Lillian Weigl. Many thanks to Katherine Relda also.

Last but not least, I am grateful to my best friend, most favorite person in the world, the man who makes me laugh, my lover, all of whom are, of course, my husband, Vincent. What a guy!

God has no hands or feet but us.
God first, spirit guides second.

—*Hilda DeLong*

CONTENTS

PREFACE

xi

INTRODUCTION

xiii

ONE

Defining Spirit Guides

1

TWO

Understanding Spirit

9

THREE

When Spirit Manifests

19

FOUR

Relatives As Guides

35

FIVE

Your Band of Personal Guides

43

SIX

Discerning Spirit

69

SEVEN
First Awareness
85

EIGHT
Phenomena
99

NINE
Not Playing Games
121

TEN
Getting Started
139

ELEVEN
Meditations for Communication
159

APPENDIX ONE
179

GLOSSARY
181

SUGGESTED READING
189

INDEX
191

PREFACE

The word "spirit" has numerous meanings. To avoid any confusion, and at the risk of sounding like a grammar teacher, allow me to explain exactly what the spirit means as I have used it throughout this book.

The capitalized word "Spirit" can be used in place of God, Goddess, Infinite Intelligence, the Source, the Creator—whatever term that relates to your personal understanding of a higher power. In this case, it is a proper noun:

Thank you, Spirit, for these blessings.

The phrase "spirit world" indicates a location by using the word as a proper noun:

Those relatives who live in the spirit world still love us.

Spirit also means the spiritual essence that has left the human body to transcend into the spirit world, a singular noun in this case:

> *I felt the presence of a spirit in the room.*
> *I knew that spirit was present in the house.*

Spirit can be a collective energy, a term used to generally label many entities who are in the spirit world, thereby being a collective noun:

> *When spirit communicates with us, we should feel*
> *grateful for the experience.*

The word "spirit" can also be an obvious plural:

> *Many spirits were present in the room.*

Therefore, depending upon how it is used in a sentence, the word "spirit" would be considered a proper noun, a singular noun, an irregular plural noun, or a plural noun.

May Spirit be with you always and in all ways!

INTRODUCTION

People's beliefs regarding the spirit world can be as diverse as the petals on a flower. Those who have experienced visitations from relatives in spirit are certain that there is another life besides the one we are living in. They have found comfort in the knowledge that their loved ones still live, albeit in a different dimension. Others who believe in the existence of spirit entities may feel that the spirit world is a doorway to enlightenment. Inside is an endless source of truth, hope, and abundant possibilities. They view communication with a spirit as a natural occurrence or a special privilege.

On the other end of the spectrum, there are the nonbelievers, who reject the concept of spirits and the idea that a dimension exists where they reside. They may even feel spirits are hocus-pocus, a delusion, or a fallacy. Nonbelievers accept only our earthly existence as reality. When the physical body ceases to function, they believe that is the end of life.

Some religions believe in spirits, but only in a saintly fashion. Fundamentalist Christians believe that to attempt communication with spirits is to solicit contact with the devil. Spiritualists, on the other hand, center their religion around communication with the spirit world.

It is my intention to enlighten and educate believers and nonbelievers, if they are willing. All that is required is a desire to entertain another thought pattern. I could think of no better source to use as a reference for a book focusing on spirits than Spiritualist mediums. Who better to share information about the spirit world than those who regularly contact spiritual entities? I am fortunate to live in a community of mediums, called the Southern Cassadaga Spiritualist Camp, in Cassadaga, Florida. Throughout the book I will refer to specific mediums by name who live in the community and were gracious enough to convey to me their personal stories, experiences, and beliefs. Other mediums mentioned who live elsewhere will be stipulated.

I also drew upon my own experiences as a medium and psychic artist to create this book. In 1985 an astrologer named Sylvia DeLong told me I should combine my mediumistic talents with my natural artistic ability. That suggestion propelled me into drawing my clients' spirit guides. Over the years I acquired valuable information about guides and the spirit world and have shared this knowledge with many people in seminars and private sessions.

I believe that we are entering a time when spirit will draw even closer to us, an era where the veil between the spirit world and the one we know on the earth plane will begin to lift somewhat and spirit communication will become commonplace. It is my desire that you learn about the fascinating world of spirit so that you will be able to find comfort and guidance through the assistance of spirits when your outer and inner worlds collide. You will discover how to ease the evolvement process in most situations by communicating with spirit. This book is your tool for communication with those who are so near, yet unseen. The following story is an example of how spirit can work to assist in your life.

In 1960 the Rev. Marie Lilla's sister passed away, leaving behind three adorable children, the oldest being six and the youngest only three months of age. The grandparents of the children encouraged Marie to marry her brother-in-law because she was so close to his children. Every time Marie saw the grandparents or talked to them on the phone, they would bring up the topic of marriage. Marie repeatedly questioned herself about the wisdom of marrying her brother-in-law. All she could think was, "I don't love this man." But the grandparents were persistent, saying, "You really should marry him because of the children." The pressure was affecting Marie greatly.

One day it occurred to Marie that maybe her sister was sending a message to her through the in-laws. Perhaps her sister really wanted her to marry this man.

Marie decided to go to church for the answer. She knelt in the back of the church and asked, "Okay, God, if I have to do this, I want it in black and white. I don't want it subtle."

All of a sudden Marie felt a tap on her shoulder. She turned around to see her sister in spirit, standing behind her, just as clear as if she were in human form. The sister told Marie, "Do not marry him. The children will be fine." Then she disappeared. This was the concrete guidance Marie was seeking.

Marie chose not to marry her brother-in-law. As a result of her decision, the grandparents took care of the children for the next two years until their father remarried. Marie later married another man and is still happily wedded.

My husband and best friend, Vincent, says, "All the answers are out there, we just have to tap into the source to receive." In the silence of meditation, we can find answers to perplexing situations when they arise. Those on the spirit side of life are always there, waiting to assist us in every endeavor, crisis, inspiration, and creation—if we just ask. It is so simple. Everything we need is just a breath away, closer than our hands and feet.

I feel blessed to live in a Spiritualist camp, surrounded by mediums. Oh, the stories they told and the incredible experiences they shared with me! Now I will share them with you.

DEFINING
SPIRIT GUIDES

What are spirit guides? Some believe they are entities sent by God to protect and guide us along our journeys here on earth. I prefer to say that they are emissaries of good, sent from the Universe, God, Goddess, Spirit, or whatever title denotes a higher power for you.

Spirit guides are spiritual entities living in a different life plane or dimension than the one we inhabit. They are not classified as masculine or feminine, although they will appear as one gender or the other simply for identification purposes. They are spirit, a pure spiritual essence, where a designated gender is nonexistent. Mediums believe the majority of guides that we communicate with have walked the earth as you and I. However, this is not an absolute. There are cases where spiritual beings are of such a high magnitude that they have never incarnated on the earth plane nor will they. Normally, though, our guiding forces have been in human form before they made the transition to the "other side of life." Since guides are emissaries of good, their mission is to convey information and guidance that will enlighten, protect, and teach through those of us who have learned how to attune to their higher vibrations.

The Rev. Dr. Warren Hoover prefers to call them spirit teachers rather than guides. He defines spirit teachers as aids or helpers from the spirit world that are drawn to us in a sense of harmony.

Another definition for spirit guides comes from the Rev. Arlene Sikora. Her personal encounter is "a vibratory light force that guides my path, that talks to me, informs me for myself and others, keeps me out of harm's way, and makes me feel lucky every once in a while. A protector, nurturer."

The Rev. Sylvia DeLong, the astrologer who advised me to draw spirit guides, calls her guiding forces spirit friends. They have told her, "We are just like you, but you can't see us."

The Rev. Diane Davis believes spirit guides are entities or intelligences that have the ability to inspire, direct, heal, encourage, and influence.

It has been proven scientifically that energy never dies. Clinically, the physical body may no longer be alive, but the energy that once existed within continues to survive. The physical body is merely a vehicle used by spirits to experience their designated time on earth. When we incarnate, it is a learning experience—a chance to work through karma, a school for our spiritual development. Once there is a cessation of physical life, the spirit evolves to the next plane of existence, the spirit world, where souls can continue to grow spiritually. Sometimes the spirit assumes the position of a spirit guide to people on earth. After all, there is no better way for our souls to advance than through service to others.

As a Spiritualist by faith and an ordained minister in the religion, I certainly believe in life after physical death. The spirits that mediums see, feel, and hear have shown that they have a purpose. They are not hovering about patiently waiting for Judgment Day. Spirits are occupying their time by busily assisting us and making the most of their opportunity to grow spiritually.

Unfortunately, traditional religions discourage us from seeking communication with the spirit world. Instead we are threatened with the potential for damnation in hell and the fear of possession by an evil spirit in order to discourage us from this activity. I believe that is inaccurate information.

For those who practice the traditional faiths, fear retribution for contacting spirits, and believe in the Bible, let me say that Jesus was a prophet, psychic, healer, and teacher. He said, according to John 14:12, "He who believes in me will also do the works that I do; and greater works than these will he do." Also, in I Cor. 12, there are a number of verses discussing spiritual gifts. The passage states that there are a variety of gifts that we may be blessed with and all are inspired by God. It goes on to name many of these spiritual gifts given by God, such as healing, prophecy, and distinguishing between spirits.

I cannot find anything negative, fearful, or inappropriate in any of these biblical passages that would cause anyone to think that it was anything but a blessing to receive gifts from God. The phrase "gifts from God" has only positive connotations. There is nothing forbidden, frightening, or insinuating retribution within that phrase. Therefore, one could conclude that contacting the spirit world has God's approval. That is certainly my conclusion.

Articles have been published where the Roman Catholic Church has stated that some of its priests share a belief in communication with the dead. A theological commentator for the Vatican newspaper stated that communication is possible between those who live on earth and those who are in spirit. He further conveyed a belief that our loved ones send us messages to guide us during periods in our lives, frequently influence our impulses and inspiration, and appear in dreams.

Examples of spirit communication and manifestation can be found throughout the Bible and in other religious texts. One of my favorites is 1 Sam. 28:7:

Then said Saul unto his servants, "Seek me a
woman that hath a familiar spirit, that I may
go to her and enquire of her." And his servants
said to him, "Behold, there is a woman that
hath a familiar spirit at Endor."

Saul made this request because God had not answered him, neither by dreams, nor by Urim, nor by prophets. So he sought the services of a medium, the medium of Endor. The verses go on to say how King Saul disguised his identity because he had cut off those that have familiar spirits, and the wizards, out of the land. The King assured the reluctant medium, "As the Lord liveth, there shall no punishment happen to thee for this thing." The medium asked, "Whom shall I bring up unto thee?" Saul said, "Bring me up Samuel." The woman produced the spirit of Samuel who gave a shocking message to Saul.[1]

Far and away, too much conclusive information has been published regarding the continued existence of people after earthly death for me to ever believe anything else except that we do truly live on. I have also personally witnessed too many incidents, and have been told of far more by other people who have been touched by those from the spirit side of life, to doubt the reality of spirits and a spirit world. Once communication is established, it makes a believer out of a "doubting Thomas" quickly. The proof is there for those who seek the answers, forever giving the doubter comfort in the knowledge of life after death and the existence of spirits.

Spirit communication can be received from friends, relatives, spouses, and personal spirit guides. And can't we all use a little help now and then during times of distress? Of course we can, and the spirit world is only too happy to assist.

Communicating with spirit entities can be beneficial in every aspect of our lives, from the mundane to the spiritual. For example, the Rev. Patti Aubrey inherited a beautiful diamond watch from her mother. Whenever she traveled, Patti always placed the valuable watch in a safe deposit box. After returning from a trip, she went to the bank to retrieve her watch, as was her custom. While in the safe deposit room, spirit told her very clearly, "Put the watch on." Patti ignored the suggestion. Spirit became very insistent, "Put the watch on now." Patti still ignored the prodding from spirit. They told her one final time, "Put the watch on your wrist." Patti continued to ignore the advice and tossed the watch into her purse instead. When she got into her car, she became concerned because of all the insisting from spirit, so Patti searched through her purse for the precious watch. It wasn't there. Patti flew back into the bank and into the safe deposit area. Her watch was nowhere to be found. It had simply vanished. If Patti had paid attention to the advice of spirit, she would have her watch today.

If you are open to the concept of spirit communication, or are already a believer, this book will assist you in your quest for knowledge about your spirit friends and loved ones.

Notes

1. For your convenience, I have listed numerous examples that can be found in the Bible. If you have a desire to investigate further, you will find these examples helpful.

    Gen. 18:1–16

    Ezek. 3:14; 3:24

    Acts 2:4; 4:31; 6:10; 8:29; 8:39; 9:3–9; 10:10; 12:4–12; 16:9

    Luke 1:28–30; 2:25–29; 24:13–31

    Matt. 4:1; 13:16–17; 24:29–31; 26:1

    Exod. 24:12–16

    Rev. 1:10

TWO

UNDERSTANDING SPIRIT

One school of thought teaches that each individual has seven spirit guides. All the mediums I interviewed disagreed with this concept, stating that this was an antiquated philosophy. Each medium thought we would be placing a limitation on spiritual communication by accepting such a regulated approach, especially since the spirit world is endless and each of us has free will.

Because seven is a mystical number, it is conceivable that at some period it was determined that seven was the specific number of spirit guides one would possess. The Rev. Diane Davis feels that the seven chakras might also have played a part in creating the initial teaching of seven guides, with each guide corresponding to a particular chakra. Sylvia DeLong commented that during our earthly lives we acquire more than seven friends, so it would be logical for us to have more than seven guiding spirits looking out for our welfare.

We do not receive all of our guides at birth. The gatekeeper is the only guide a baby comes into this world with. (You will read more about the gatekeeper and other specific guides in chapter 5.) During childhood there are "inactive guides" waiting in the wings, so to speak, while other guides perform important duties that are pertinent to the child at that particular period of growth. As the child matures, he or she may become more aware of the other guides as their influence is exhibited.

Children are very aware of spirits of all kinds and relations. They are so close to the other side that their young souls have not yet been contaminated by the earthly world, nor have their memories faded away completely. Their sensitivity is keen to the vibration of spirit entities, but, unfortunately, will probably be lost through conditioning. At the age of three, though, it is common for children to tell their parents something similar to this:

"Mommie, why is Uncle George standing there on the front porch?"

"No one is on the porch, Johnny," replies the mother, glancing over her shoulder at the screened door. She does not see anyone standing on the other side of the door on their porch.

"Yes, he is," Johnny insists. "He's waving at me."

"Uncle George died last week, remember, Johnny?" Mother continues, "You are just imagining he is standing there because you miss him."

If Johnny persists, his mother will tell him whatever it takes to banish this notion from his little head. Eventually, Johnny will no longer be able to see spirits and will forget that he ever could—thus, conditioning. Unfortunately, as we mature, we grow farther away from the spiritual cords that connected us to spirit when we were young, and our lives become more inclined to the material elements of our existence. However, if we become interested in meditation and communication with the spirit world, we can re-open the lines of communication through meditative practice.

Spirit guides form what is commonly referred to as a band, which is the collective group of individual guides. As adults, those who seek to be reunited with their spirit teachers may or may not be aware of all of their guides at the same time. Total awareness of every single guide really isn't an important issue or necessary for your well-being and spiritual development. Due to circumstances in our lives, one guide may be dominant. When change occurs, subtle or dramatic, one guide frequently becomes more prominent than the others. Several could take a back seat to a few dominant guides due to family and work circumstances. Then when cycles in a life change, the less active ones once again regain prominence, or a whole new set could come in.

As our lives change due to maturity and circumstances of life, our guides also change. I often say to clients, "What could your first grade teacher teach you now? Hopefully, not much of anything." We do not retain all of our original guides throughout our lives. We eventually will require a more learned instructor at some point. A different spirit energy becomes necessary to continue growth because we have outgrown a guide's area of expertise. The guide then moves on to another person and guides him or her in the same manner within that field. This statement is not meant to diminish the guide's value, but to show that they all work within the boundary of their learning. As an example, some years ago when Sylvia DeLong and her father, Leland, asked their spirit guides about reincarnation, they were told that the guides did not know of such things. Eventually, another spirit who was familiar with the subject revealed information about reincarnation to them.

A guide may give direction within its area of expertise to several people in a row. When the guide has sufficiently completed this learning experience, the entity will begin to direct others on more advanced levels. We never stop growing, especially when we are in spirit. Just as we progress in our development as humans, spirits evolve on the spirit side of life as well. As above, so below. They are working to uplift their vibrations on the other side so they may draw closer to God. To do this, they continue their spiritual education by learning from higher beings than themselves while they are assisting us here on earth. As they become more advanced, they influence people appropriate to their particular level of development.

Spirit guides do not change every year. Many people I have spoken with have had some of their guides for twenty or forty years. The Rev. Lillian Weigl has been guided by her principle guide, Jerry, for fifty-two years. He first came to her during a meditation, stating, "Hello, my name is Jerry and I'm going to be with you a long time." He appeared as a big man with a beard and a receding hairline, possessing large hands and feet, and dressed in buckskins. When Jerry appears currently, so many years later, he wears a gray calico shirt with a small stand-up collar. Jerry is always present during Lillian's readings, frequently when she meditates, and on a more mundane level in the course of the day. They have formed a special relationship and an enduring one.

The guide Jeff came to Louis Gates when Louis was three years old. He is now forty-seven. Jeff looks to be about thirty-five years of age, according to Louis, with black hair combed back from his face, blue eyes, and an olive complexion. Jeff usually wears a suit and claims that he has been with Louis always and will continue to be for all eternity. Louis feels that they are twin souls, soulmates, having been together for many incarnations. Jeff appears to be Louis' gatekeeper guide, because he is the one who allows other entities to communicate with Louis during readings.

The amount of time that a guide gives in service to an individual appears to depend on the guide's karma and the individual's karma. If certain elements in a person's life do not change, the guide probably will not either.

Past Lives with a Spirit Guide

I have experienced many cases where there has been a past-life connection between a client and one of his or her guides. One case in particular comes to mind. After I drew a woman's spirit guide, it turned out that she had been her elder sister in a past life. In the former life, after the two sisters were orphaned, the older of the two felt responsible for the younger sibling. Unfortunately, the elder sister died, leaving the younger one to struggle through to adulthood the best way she could. The spirit of the older sister had such a strong sense of responsibility that she felt compelled to be a guiding force to the younger sister even as the sibling's spirit had reincarnated into the present lifetime.

Another example would be a guide named Henry James, who assists a person I will call Doris. They shared a previous life together in sixteenth-century England as husband and wife. He was an English nobleman. She was of Scottish ancestry. Doris talks of recollections of Queen Elizabeth I from that incarnation. Whenever Henry is around, she feels very English and a little out of touch with her surroundings, as if she were a temporary visitor from that country. She attributes her fascination today with English royalty to this past life experience as a nobleman's wife in England.

Sylvia DeLong had a wonderful experience about past life connections, spirit guides, and the Toltec Indians. A whole series of events showed Sylvia how we can have guides attracted to us from our past incarnations. When Sylvia was an adult, she was told by spirit about a previous incarnation in Mexico where she had been an advisor to the high priest of the Toltec Indians. Sylvia felt this explained her keen interest in Mexico since childhood and her desire to visit that country. Later, when Sylvia researched this information, she discovered that the Toltec Indians practiced a highly evolved astrological system. Sylvia realized then that this past life would have also contributed to her interest in astrology and subsequent career as an astrologer. During meditation, she was given further information that she would have had an association with a Mexican pyramid, and that the name of Cholula was connected to this experience in her past life. The meaning of this spirit message would be revealed to Sylvia later.

While conducting a retreat in Georgia, Sylvia met a Toltec Indian. The Indian took quite an interest in her and eventually said, "You have to come with me. I am taking you home. I have to show you this pyramid where you were." But Sylvia had no intention of going anywhere with a strange man.

Sylvia eventually had the opportunity to visit Mexico with two friends. Because it felt so familiar, she returned many times. On one of the return trips she took her parents. Upon looking at a guide book, she discovered that there was a tour that went to the Toltec Indians' Pyramids of Cholula. Naturally, the family had to participate in that tour. Sylvia felt a true bonding with that location when they visited. All the information spirit had told her then fell into place.

One of Sylvia's current spirit friends is a Toltec Indian named Kola. He calls Sylvia his savior because the Toltecs practiced human sacrifice, and Sylvia was able to save him from death because she was a high priestess in the former life. He is devoted to her forever and has said, "A feather will be my sign."

To prove this, when Sylvia and her mother visited Europe, they occasionally found feathers placed in areas for the purpose of giving them a secure feeling, like they were being looked after. While visiting a castle in Scandinavia, Sylvia's mother, Hilda, went to the restroom, which was located around the back of the dungeon area. She felt rather uncomfortable being alone behind the castle, until she saw a black feather near the door. Hilda took this as a sign of protection. When they were in Hungary, another black feather was seen. In England, at the entrance to a country inn at Avon on Gorge, they saw a white feather. All of these feather appearances they attributed to Kola.

Sharing Guides

It is possible to share a guide with someone else. Connie, a friend of mine, and her husband jointly communicate with their shared spirit teacher during nightly meditations. I also know of two sets of twins who share a spirit guide.

The best example, though, of sharing guides would be the DeLong family. During the years when both Sylvia DeLong's parents were living, her family consistently shared certain guides. Dr. Sawyer was one such spirit friend. He first came to Sylvia's father, Leland DeLong, in the 1940s as his main teacher and guide, promising to help Leland write his weekly sermons. Early in the relationship with the family, Dr. Sawyer communicated that he was a Church of England priest and that he loved astrology. He instructed Leland to purchase astrology books written by Sepharial because he had studied under Sepharial. When they purchased the books, Leland and Sylvia both loved them; one reason being, they were written in an Old English style, which Dr. Sawyer obviously realized would appeal to both of them.

Dr. Sawyer had instructed Leland to set aside one day a week in which to write his sermons and to do nothing else. One week his wife, Hilda, got him off track, and when Saturday rolled around, he had no sermon prepared for Sunday. Hilda had to beg Dr. Sawyer to come help her husband. Dr. Sawyer scolded the family, saying, "We (spirits) come a long way and we work hard with you and you must do as we instruct." Leland never again failed to set aside that one day a week for sermon writing.

Dr. Sawyer helped Sylvia with her sermons after Leland stopped delivering them, setting Thursdays aside for her sermon work. Even if she didn't have an idea for a sermon when she sat down to write, she found that the ideas would always come with Dr. Sawyer's assistance. He is still with her today, even though she no longer chooses to speak publicly.

You will find that there are many adventures ahead for you as you investigate the world of spirit. So many opportunities and experiences await your seeking mind—and the happenings just keep evolving. Spirit will continually surprise you with interesting moments and wonderful inspirations. We never stop growing during our earth walk, and that is especially true when we communicate with spirit. It is an avenue rich with potential and chock-full of delights!

THREE

WHEN SPIRIT MANIFESTS

You will find that spirits have interesting ways of making their presence known. Sometimes communication announcements are subtle, such as a touch, a tickle on the cheek, a tap on the shoulder or arm, or the feeling of a hand resting on the shoulder. For the very blessed, spirit will manifest in the physical, right before their eyes. Spirits may also appear as if we are seeing them "in our head." Sensing the presence of spirit teachers is an announcement of their arrival and hearing spirit voices is yet another. Allow me to explain in more depth.

The first time I sought the services of a medium, I was directed to a lady named Ruth Callin in Orlando, Florida. Her primary guide was named Star, and when Star wanted to make her presence known, she would gently tug on a piece of hair on the top of Ruth's head.

When Rabbi Lieberman comes to the Rev. Lillian Weigl, she sees him out of the corner of her eye, bowing from the waist with his hands placed in front of his chest in a prayerful position. Rabbi Lieberman is heavyset in appearance, according to Lillian, with dark gray hair and big, impressionable eyes.

The spirits in Sylvia DeLong's band let her know they want to communicate by giving her chills all over her body. If she ignores the signal, they will increase the intensity of the chills. It is like they are insisting, "This is the time." Sylvia then sits down to meditate.

The Rev. Marie Lilla says that her cheeks itch when she is doing a reading. She likes to think of it as receiving lots of little spirit kisses.

When the Rev. Arlene Sikora's spiritual advisors are around, they make their presence known by her seeing, what is called in this work, spirit lights. In other words, she literally sees lights. The lights appear around or over the clients' heads and are separate from their aura. The spirit lights come through individually in the colors of turquoise, purple, cobalt blue, and white. When they blend together, Arlene says the "counsel" is talking. It is a group energy, a master force, a collective consciousness. In other words, it is powerful. The spirit lights connect with her client's entities who wish to be recognized or who have a desire to give a message to the one receiving the reading. Sometimes they come in to introduce a guide to the client and give a message. The Rev. Sikora's spirit lights also come through when she is in private meditation and also randomly, with no forewarning, as she goes about her day. The spirits have not identified titles with the color of the lights or said anything as direct as, "I'm your master teacher." Apparently, it is not important for her to know. Arlene does not feel that these beings in the collective light-force have incarnated, whereas she knows that some other presences that work with her in mundane areas have been connected with an earth vibration at one time.

I have found that all students want to be able to see their spirit teachers and relations. This ability is called clairvoyance, which is the French word for "clear seeing." The term "seeing," in rare cases, means literally "seeing spirit with the physical eyes." This ability usually begins during early childhood and is called objective clairvoyance. Louis Gates sees his guides and other entities actually sit down beside him when he gives a reading.

It is more common, though, for people to be in a meditative state viewing images with closed eyes, termed "seeing" with the third eye. This is subjective clairvoyance. Colors are usually the first experience a beginning student will encounter, followed by symbols, before they experience the image of a spirit. The spirit may appear hazy in form, in full figure, or perhaps only the face or hands will be seen.

Another example of subjective clairvoyance would be when a medium briefly sees small spirit faces appear around the client's head during a reading. The medium isn't actually seeing them physically with his or her eyes, but rather receiving impressions while the eyes are open. I would liken this to listening to your friend while she describes her experiences on a skiing trip, for instance, and being able to vividly picture what she is describing. Your eyes are wide open, but you are "seeing" images.

It is important to stress that everyone is an individual and develops in his or her own unique way. The examples that I give are what are considered a common development pattern in our collective experiences as teachers. But spirit may choose to communicate with you in a different manner. They may impress you with symbols, intended for your interpretation, rather than allowing themselves to be seen. Some mediums work strictly with this form of communication and do not see spirits at all, receiving by impression instead.

Symbols can be tricky. Although symbols are usually meant for interpretation by the recipient, a client may decipher a different meaning of a symbol when a medium is giving a reading. Occasionally, symbols will be relayed to the client by the medium and are meant as a specific message that only the client will understand. Most developed mediums see symbols during readings and meditations in addition to receiving through other forms of communication.

All your guides and spirit friends may not choose to manifest through clairvoyance. They have other options. You may receive communication by sound, which would mean you are blessed with clairaudient talents. Clairaudience means "clear hearing," which enables you to hear the voices of your guides or other sounds, such as a train or animals. Again, these sounds may be very clear and literal, as if hearing music on the radio or the sound of a human voice speaking.

The subtler sounds are more common, though. It would be similar to experiencing a song that keeps running through your head or a name or word repeatedly popping into your thoughts. However, I don't mean to suggest that every time you notice a song persistently in your thoughts, a spirit is trying to convey a message. Some mediums, though, do hear songs in their heads during readings that have meaning for the clients or lines in lyrics will be significant. Sylvia DeLong says that it is like hearing a voice inside her head, and when it is strong and persistent, she pays attention.

Another way spirit communicates with Sylvia is by calling out the name Suzie. Sylvia was called Suzie as a child, so when she hears the name Suzie spoken from spirit, she knows Dr. Sawyer or Dr. Medford has something to say to her. When Sylvia hears the endearing phrase, My Lassie, she knows it is Harry, a Scottish psychiatrist friend of hers, who she assisted with the writing of a book on astral psychiatry when he was on the earth plane. So, again, she knows to stop what she is doing and meditate. In each case, she knows who wants to speak to her.

On occasion, Sylvia has literally heard sounds from spirit. Prior to her father's passing, Leland DeLong would thump his cane on the floor beside his bed to summon assistance from his wife or daughter. Leland eventually passed away one day at 2 P.M. Shortly after retiring for bed on the evening of her beloved father's passing to spirit, Sylvia distinctly heard the "thump, thump, thump" of his cane in her bedroom. She knew he was telling her that he was present in her room. Sylvia now experiences a little tapping movement on her pillow at night when she is feeling a bit low. She interprets this to be a message from her father intended to cheer her up.

The Rev. Patti Aubrey has literally heard voices since around the age of five. When she moved to Florida, the sounds became stronger. Spirit informed her, "We are going to help you." When Patti later purchased a motor home park, the voices proved to be true to their word. They told her who to rent to, where to go to buy things, and alerted her to problems within the park before they became obvious. She has never been able to distinguish whether it is a male or female voice that speaks to her, only that it is very distinctive.

A couple of years ago, Patti's ability to hear spirit took a new twist. She had a remarkable experience when she visited Oregon, where nature spirits began speaking to her, mostly through the trees. It happened one morning when she was enjoying a stroll around a mountain and came to a grove. One of the trees surprised her by saying, "I am love and you may hug me." The tree beside the first one said to Patti, "I am wisdom and you may not touch me yet."

This was a moving experience for Patti and also became the start of other trees communicating with her. When she returned home, Patti found that her backyard trees began to talk to her. "I'm choking," one said. Upon examining the tree more closely, she found that vines were wrapped around it, so Patti cut the vines away to enable the tree to breathe. Some of Patti's plants will even tell her when they need water.

Developing mediums frequently hear spirits calling their names at unexpected times outside of meditation. As a developing medium I once had that experience as I lay on the couch watching television. I heard my name as clear as the proverbial bell, and I was sure I knew who the person was on the other side of the door. When I swung open the door, no one was there. And no one was walking down the hallway either. I never received an explanation for this. Perhaps spirit was testing me to see if I would respond.

Another form of communication is clairsentience, which means "clear sensing." It is the ability to feel the presence of spirit or receive impressions. The best way to explain this is to give the example of two people having a terrible argument in a room. After they leave and someone else enters the room, this person feels an unexplainable uneasiness. The vibrations in the room have been disturbed—disharmony is present. It just doesn't feel right.

We have all experienced tension within a room full of agitated people, such as when we go to a meeting where people are having a dispute with the school board, for instance. I once had a distressing feeling when I passed by a closet in an old house. Later I found out that a child had been abused and locked in the closet as punishment. All these are examples of clairsentience.

We could also liken clairsentience to intuition—that gut feeling that something is wrong and we shouldn't be doing what we are about to do. If we are wise and listen to our intuition, we may find that we narrowly avoid an accident. On the other hand, we could receive an intuitive flash that indicates what we are doing is correct, despite what everyone else is advising at the time. Something inside just feels right about the situation, and you intuitively know it is the correct move.

Nancy Mostad, who works for Llewellyn Publications, heard a voice telling her not to go to work one morning. She also had "the most peculiar feeling of dread." After going about her normal routine and being unable to shake the feeling of dread, Nancy called into work, stating that she was taking a personal day, which was completely out of character for her. After three cups of coffee, Nancy's guilty conscience got the better of her. She declared aloud, "This is stupid. I'm going to work today."

Nancy placed her cup in the sink and started up the stairs to get ready for work. Suddenly from the garage came a horrendous "BANG!" that shook the whole house. Nancy timidly entered the garage from the kitchen entryway to find that the spring to the garage door had snapped. She attempted to open the door, but realized it was impossible. Nancy could not go to work that day.

Later that evening, Nancy's husband tried to replace the spring on the garage door. To his amazement, he discovered that the cable that moves the door up and down had also snapped—in five places! Nancy firmly believes that her guides saved her from some horrible fate that day.

Clairsentience also helps us to feel the presence of spirit standing behind us or beside us. It might feel as if we are being watched from behind or like an energy is standing close by. The Rev. Steve Hermann is a medium from Massachusetts who comes to serve our church in Cassadaga periodically. Steve told me that he feels as if a group of spirits are working with him when he gives readings, sensing them standing just behind his back.

The Rev. Dr. Warren Hoover feels the presence of one guide in particular when he works in a public forum giving messages or in a private setting during a reading. The spirit teacher he senses is Dr. Henry, who was an Episcopal minister who lived in Massachusetts during the 1800s. Dr. Henry came through for the first time during a séance that H. Gordon Burroughs was conducting when Warren was studying to be a medium. Mr. Burroughs was a well-known Spiritualist medium at that time, who wrote the book *Becoming a Spiritualist* in 1962.

Clairgustance, the French word for "clear smelling," is the ability to smell spirit. Yes, spirits really can emit a fragrance! (Let's hope yours chooses a pleasant one.) When Lillian Weigl moved into her current house, she had quite a time with a spirit that inhabited it. One night she came home and discovered her upstairs level reeking of urine, and it wasn't coming from the bathroom. She couldn't find anything amiss. This happened several times. She consulted another medium who lived next door at the time, asking if anyone had ever lived in the house who might have had a bladder or kidney problem. The other medium told her that, yes, there had been someone fitting that description. That night she addressed the spirit, assuming it could hear her, saying, "If you want to manifest, talk, that's fine, but not with that odor." He was a stubborn spirit and did not leave or change his habits easily. Then one night during the heat of summer, she awoke with her head resting on her arm and noticed the arm smelled strongly of urine. Lillian demanded, "Mister, why are you doing that here? Don't you ever come into this room again." She went into the bathroom and showered to relieve herself of the smell. The spirit never returned.

Normally, spirits manifest by the scent of perfume, cigarettes, or cigars. If, for instance, your grandmother always wore lily of the valley perfume, and after her death you smelled that same fragrance in a room for no explainable reason, I would feel she was trying to identify herself to you through that aroma, so you would know she was present in spirit. This is common for spirits to do. When my father was on the earth plane, he smoked cigarettes, and when he manifests, I can smell the odor of a burning cigarette. I once was strolling through an outdoor art show in Winter Park, Florida. Suddenly, I became aware of the smell of smoke from a cigarette. I knew no one was allowed to smoke around the paintings at the art show, and I could see no one breeching the rules around me. My dad was always proud of my artistic ability and encouraged me to draw, so I knew it was my father expressing his approval of me being at the art show.

One other even stranger note: I have no sense of smell, but I can smell spirit. I literally smell whatever odor spirit is sending. I often ask my husband, Vincent, if he smells an odor, and invariably he will say he does not, and he happens to have a good sense of smell. Under those circumstances, I know it is a spirit present.

It is important to pay attention to the synchronicity of events in our lives. Some may view synchronistic happenings as a coincidence, but nothing happens by coincidence. There is purpose and intention in all events, and we can prove this to ourselves simply by paying a little attention to what is occurring around us. When we choose to ignore events or dismiss an intended lesson as just a coincidence, we are missing an opportunity to grow. Synchronistic events are just another subtle way that spirit has of communicating information to us.

The Rev. Diane Davis is especially aware of syn-chronicity in her life. I will share one such incident with you that, as I was taping her interview, brought on yet another example.

Diane had entered into a new relationship and was experiencing fear because she had opened herself up to be emotionally vulnerable. She was anxious to do all the right things that would make the relationship work. One night, after being intimate in an unfamiliar house, Diane crept out to the living room around 2 or 3 A.M. While she was lying on the couch, crying over her fears, a cat came over and lay down on Diane's chest. Then the grandfather clock chimed in the house, and when it did, she felt as if someone were squeezing her cheek, just like her grandfather did when he was alive. It was one of his endearing ges-tures. The grandfather clock chiming was also signifi-cant because this was always how he made his presence known to her from spirit. She received the words in her mind, "Everything is going to be all right. Go back to bed." And with that she felt very peaceful and went back to the bedroom. Four months later she was diag-nosed with a brain tumor and was told that the right side of her face had been numb for quite awhile. Even though her face would have been numb during her grandfather's spirit visit, unbeknownst to her at the time, Diane had felt her grandfather squeeze her cheek.

Now, to add to this synchronicity story: While Diane was sharing this incident with me and said, "Then the grandfather clock chimed," at that very moment my grandfather clock began to chime! We had a good chuckle over that.

One morning I asked spirit to give me direction about whether or not to pursue a particular writing project. That same afternoon I was driving to Daytona Beach on Interstate 4 with the radio blasting away. As I was about to make my exit, former Beatle George Harrison began singing *I Got My Mind Set On You*. During the chorus he kept repeating "Do it, do it, do it, do it." At the exact time he was singing the "do it" portion, a motorcyclist passed me on the left side. Printed in large black letters on the back of his T-shirt were the words "Do It." So, I did it! The message here: Pay attention to synchronistic events.

Your guides and spirit relations may communicate with you in one manner only or in several. All the mediums I interviewed for this book receive spirit communication in more than one way. It is likely that you will, too. I would expect that when you become acquainted with three guides, you will find that each communicates differently. One of your guides may choose to communicate through symbols only, while another, for instance, may both speak to you and appear on occasion. Clairsentience, though, is the one ability that everyone possesses and can develop more strongly.

The choice is theirs and the gift is yours. These talents you exhibit—clairvoyance, clairaudience, clairsentience, and clairgustance—are gifts from God. Respect them as such. Do not abuse them. These blessings can be taken away. Always use your gifts for the benefit of yourself and others.

Bud Dickinson, his wife, and another couple went on a canoe trip on the Moose River in the Adirondack Mountains, near Old Forge, New York. All four were in the canoe, with Bud paddling in front. A friend, Anne Haughton, seated right behind Bud, took this picture, intending to capture the beauty of the scenic river. Instead, when the picture was developed, they saw something on the back of his shirt (bottom right). At first it looks like a head of hair, but the only person directly behind him was the photographer. Taking a closer look at this swirling, wavy area, a spirit face appears. Bud and his friends think it looks like a woman, possibly Native American, holding both hands up to her face. They have no explanation for this appearance.

FOUR

RELATIVES
AS GUIDES

M any people who believe in spirit guides and have the sensitivity to feel the presence of a relative in spirit have a tendency to feel that this relative is a personal guide. This may or may not be true, but, as a rule, relatives are not usually our guides.

It is a natural conclusion, though, to believe that our relatives, parents, spouses, and friends who have made the transition to the other side can and want to become our guides. If a person happens to be very sensitive, he or she may unexpectedly receive a visit from a recently departed member of the family. If that person believes in the existence of spirit guides prior to the visitation, he or she may automatically jump to the conclusion that "Aunt Ellie" is a new guiding force.

In healthy families, it is normal for parents to help their children by providing guidance, comfort, and assistance. It would be illogical to think that parents suddenly would be unwilling to help simply because they were not in the physical world. When in spirit, they continue to love, they continue to care. Their feelings have not changed because they have crossed over to the spirit world. The bonds between a child and parent are especially strong, not unlike an umbilical cord from the spirit world to the earth plane. Parents would certainly manifest in spirit to lend guidance or to share in a joyous experience with a child on earth. But that doesn't automatically mean they are spirit guides.

Our spirit relatives, friends, and spouses cared about us, loved us, and wanted only the best things life had to offer for each of us while they were in human form. It is common for any relative to visit a loved one, especially when the loved one is distressed or during special events such as religious holidays, weddings, anniversaries, and birthdays. It should be anticipated and thought of as a natural occurrence that a spirit relative or friend would have a desire to visit during trying times and happy events.

Don, my former husband, was about twelve years old when he had his first visitation from his grandfather, shortly after the gentleman passed away. He came to Don in the middle of the night to tell him that he had died. In the morning Don was told by his mother that his grandfather had passed during the night.

Thereafter, when important events in Don's life warranted direction, his grandfather would come to him. One such occasion was shortly after I had met Don. His grandfather visited him during the night to inform Don that he was going to marry me. We were married three months later. The prediction set into motion events in my life that would eventually lead me to Cassadaga, Florida, after the marriage ended seven years later. If the grandfather had not communicated with Don, it is unlikely I would be where I am today. Was the grandfather a spirit guide to Don? I do not believe so, but this is an excellent example of how spirit relatives can assist us.

The Rev. Marie Lilla has a brother in spirit who she calls upon for assistance. One case in particular was in 1992, when Marie and her husband traveled to Italy. The couple decided to return early from their trip, but the airline could not accommodate them. They were directed to come to the airport to be on standby for a flight. Once at the airline counter, Marie began to call upon her brother, telling him how much she wanted to go home and that she needed to get on that plane.

The Lillas were sixteenth on the standby list and began to wait. Many people grew tired of waiting, so they left. Before long, the man at the counter called the Lillas' name. He told them he had room for two, and they would be seated in row number nineteen. Now, it is important to mention that the number nineteen is very significant for Marie. Her father died on the nineteenth of September at the time when this particular brother in spirit was nineteen years of age. Later, when the Lillas arrived in Greenland to make a connection, they heard that the plane had been overbooked by two people. Marie gives full credit to her brother in spirit for helping with their speedy return. Is Marie's brother a personal guide? I believe he is a very caring relative, not a guide.

Haven't we all heard of someone who is recently widowed receiving a visit from his or her partner in spirit? What could be more natural then a spouse returning in spirit form to bring comfort to a grieving loved one? I should think any widow or widower would find such an experience heartening and a confirmation of eternal life.

A friend of mine named Gracie relayed a story to me about her experiences after her husband passed away. She was having a very hard time adjusting to his passing and decided to get out the Ouija board. Gracie found no difficulty operating the Ouija board alone. With her hands placed on the pointer, it began to move about in such a manner that she knew she was not manipulating it. The experience left her feeling that she had truly communicated with her husband in spirit, because the things that came through were messages only he or she would have known. Gracie felt great consolation afterward.

Gracie then happened to read a book about automatic writing and attempted to receive communication by this method also. She felt that some of her Old English ancestors communicated with her. Two of several entities that came through were a lady organist from a church and a man who was a director of a school. Gracie felt these encounters were rewarding also. Were any of these spirits her guides? No, they were visiting spirits who brought either consolation or joy.

On occasion, people require the comforting knowledge that a deceased loved one is all right. Frequently, a person will seek out the services of a medium in order to receive this knowledge.

The Spiritualist religion became extremely popular after its inception on March 31, 1848, for this very reason. The attraction to Spiritualism was so great, especially prior to the turn of the century, because women desperately needed confirmation that their deceased children still lived. We must remember that at that time in history, women did not have any rights. They could not vote, inherit property, and were thought of as being personal possessions to be owned by a husband or father. Women were required to submit to their husband's sexual desires and, as a consequence, became pregnant year after year. (Those of you who venture into family genealogy will most likely discover eight to twelve children being ordinary occurrences in families throughout the 1800s.) Repeated pregnancies were too much of a physical strain on many women, so they did not always bear healthy children. As a result, a great number of these children did not live long. Women flocked to mediums for messages from their deceased children, hoping for any soothing words to prove their offspring still lived on in some way. These were certainly difficult times in which the voices of spirits brought immeasurable comfort to those seeking answers.

Our parents, friends, relatives, and spouses are definitely available to us for comfort and guidance, along with many other spirits than those who knew us on the earth plane. But a willingness to help does not make every one of them a spirit guide. For example, every woman blessed with a maternal instinct who shows us motherly gestures is not our mother. The visitation of a relative is usually an additional guiding force not associated with a person's regular band of spirit guides. But, there are exceptions to every rule.

Ever since Louis Gates' great-grandfather, Chief Joseph, passed to spirit, he has been keeping order within Louis' life. He brings Louis peace and understanding of situations around him. Louis, who is one-half Seneca Indian, remembers his great-grandfather wearing a full headdress. Chief Joseph still wears a full headdress, even in spirit, as a means to identify himself to Louis.

Another example would be that of Eloise Page, who came to Cassadaga, Florida, in 1948. She studied mediumship with a gentleman named E. B. Page, who later became her husband. E. B. was Eloise's mentor and groomed her into the fine medium she became. When he passed to the spirit side of life, the spirit of E. B.

assumed the role of Eloise's teacher guide. This would have been a natural position for him, in particular, to assume. No one could have been better to serve as her teacher than the man who was instrumental in her spiritual development. But again, these examples are not common occurrences.

FIVE

YOUR BAND OF PERSONAL GUIDES

S pirit guides influence many areas of our lives, such as professions, talents, and spirituality. Whatever area the spirit is familiar with from one of their incarnations on earth is the area in which the influence will be felt. The same is true for spirits in general, because they all retain their personal characteristics when they make their transition into spirit. If they were mathematically astute, artistically gifted, hot-tempered, or generous to a fault, they are the same in spirit. I always like to use my father and aunt as examples.

My dad was a businessman. He had an ability with money matters and finances. On the other hand, one of his sisters was a bit of a ding-a-ling when she was on the earth plane and could have cared less about financial matters. Considering that we retain our personalities when we cross over into the spirit world, when I need assistance in money matters, who do you think I call on? My dad, of course. My aunt would not be capable of communicating anything of worth about finances. Now, spending money—that's another story!

When Patti Aubrey first moved to Florida, she purchased a mobile home park. As the owner, it was necessary for her to do the bookkeeping. Unfortunately, this was not an area where she was very accomplished. One night she was so frustrated, she called upon her mother in spirit for help. She said, "Ma, if you're not too busy, could you come help me?"

Patti's mother had been the head bookkeeper for the Boston Redevelopment Authority. When Patti asked her for assistance, her mother responded, "Patti, it's this column. And this is what you have to do . . . ." Patti's mother answered all her questions so thoroughly that she never had to ask for help thereafter.

Spirit guides with similar characteristics are drawn to us. Frequently they will share the same interests, possess similar personality traits, and may have been in the same profession as we are. Somewhere within this union there are going to be similarities.

The most prominent spirit entity I felt around one particular lady was a doctor guide. As it turned out, she was a veterinarian. I have found that doctor guides and Native American medicine people are frequently associated with those who work within the healing professions, especially nurses. The master teacher seems to come in when I am asked to draw for highly religious people. I could name many examples, but you see what I am saying. We attract to us that which is similar.

The following descriptions of individual guides are meant to be a format to work from and not intended to be an absolute. The use of titles is for identification purposes, not a decree. So please, use the following information as a guideline to distinguish between the influence you experience and area of guidance received from one spirit guide and another.

The Gatekeeper

The first guide in the band is called the gatekeeper or doorkeeper. I have also heard the term life guide used. This particular spirit teacher is with you from birth until you make your transition to spirit. The gate-keeper is the overall protector. This spirit looks out for your best interests and holds you close so no harm may come to you. Very often when I see a gatekeeper around a client, the guide will stand behind the person, wearing a voluminous cape, which the guide wraps around the individual. Sometimes the guide will be dressed in clothing with lots of enveloping folds, such as a gown with yards of fabric in the skirt. This auto-matically signals to me a feeling of protection and quickly identifies the guide as the gatekeeper.

Malcomb is my gatekeeper. He appears as an older, wise gentleman, with glowing white hair and beautiful blue eyes twinkling above his white beard. He usually presents himself dressed in a hooded cape, appearing quite dignified in his demeanor—regal, actually. Besides affording general protection, he gives personal guidance in most matters, except health, and assists somewhat with my writing. I am his child, and he looks after me in a parental way since I have no living parents.

Another function of the gatekeeper is to oversee the other members in the band. This also can be extended to spirits who wish to communicate with a medium. Frequently it is the gatekeeper who allows or disallows a client's spirit people to come into a reading being given by a medium. The gatekeeper is a primary guide, always there to protect and lend guidance. While some of your guides may change periodically, this life guide is a constant companion. It is especially true for the gatekeeper to find similar personality characteristics as your own.

The Doctor Guide

The doctor guide, also referred to as the physician, is most prominent in a person's life when they work as a healing professional, such as a nurse, doctor, chiropractor, veterinarian, or spiritual healer. I have found that it is especially common for nurses, in particular, to consciously channel healing to their patients. Although most of the nurses I came in contact with were not metaphysical thinkers or trained to channel healing, such as in the case of a spiritual healer, each person told me that they felt they were channeling spiritual healing to their patients. Each claimed that their source was an undefined spiritual influence.

Some people who work in traditional medical professions, however, are keenly aware that a particular spirit is influencing the healing process. When I was drawing a spirit guide for a woman five years ago, a very strong physician guide came through that worked with this individual. The woman turned out to be a veterinarian and expressed to me her awareness of this spiritual influence since childhood, when she first became attracted to the animal kingdom and felt a "calling" to come to the aid of all animals. This calling was the physician guide making its influence known to her and the beginning of the spirit working through her.

Spiritual healers, people who use tools such as crystals for healing, and any other spiritually oriented healer usually channel healing from their individual guides or state that they feel the healing comes from God. Marie Gates is a phenomenal healer who, besides channeling healing from God, also employs "angel dolls" in her healing work. Under the direction of spirit, she uses different kinds of fabric to design huggable angels with soft wings. The love she channels into the creation of her angels is felt by each recipient. Children, the elderly, and every age in-between have received the huggable

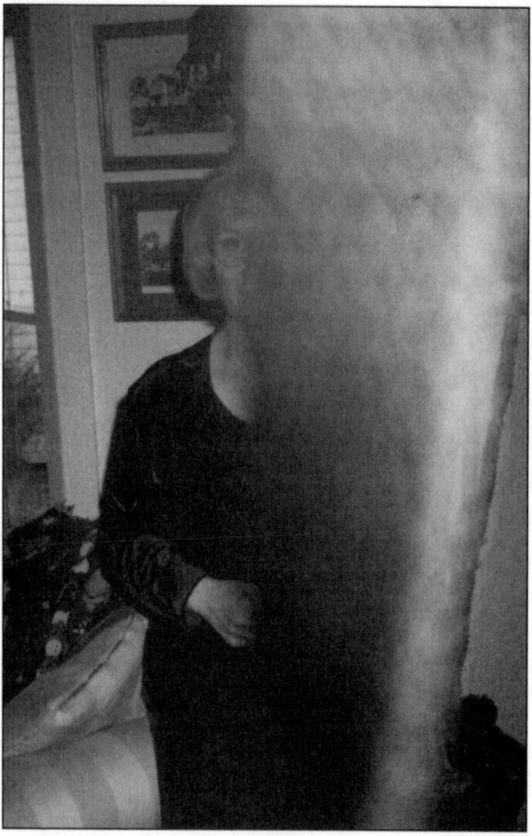

Marie Wilson Gates, a certified healer, was in the dining room of her home in Cassadaga, Florida, when her husband, Louis, also a certified healer and medium, took this photograph with an ordinary camera. Marie had expressed a desire to see what her spirit guide looked like just before Louis took the picture. Within this cone of spirit energy, Marie and Louis see wings and a heart. They believe this to be a picture of one of Marie's guides.

healing effects from Marie's angels. Marie feels that she is creating an emotionally and physically comforting doll that will attract a person's guardian angel so that he or she feels the love, protection, and healing that his or her personal angel has to offer. Many times the dolls have helped to cure the incurable or eased someone's transition from the physical world into the spirit side of life. Marie has experienced many joyous, sad, and humorous situations involving her angels. Let me share one with you.

Several years ago, Marie and her husband, Louis, were employed in a nursing home as nurses' assistants. Marie was particularly fond of one lady who was dying from breast cancer. I will call her Sarah. Marie frequently went into Sarah's room because, for some reason, the woman was reluctant to push the call button that would bring assistance. Marie told her repeatedly not to wait so long to ring the call button, that she didn't need to be in pain unnecessarily. When Marie checked on Sarah, she would often channel healing by placing her hands above the woman's chest, releasing a warm, soothing feeling to the affected area. Sarah was very appreciative of Marie for doing this.

While visiting Sarah, Marie would often regale her with inspiring happenings that usually transpired when a person received one of her angel dolls. The patient loved Marie's angel stories. One day Sarah asked Marie to make her an angel. Marie thought this was a good idea, because she felt it would bring Sarah's personal angel close to her, and perhaps she would even see it. The day Marie gave her the angel, Sarah hugged it to her chest and soon thereafter began to describe to Marie what her personal angel looked like. Marie could not see the angel herself but felt the presence in the room. It wasn't long before the woman's spirit left her body to join her guardian angel. Marie then left the room to notify someone of the lady's passing.

A short time after Sarah's transition, while Marie was at the nurses station, she was surprised to see the call light blinking on the panel, signaling a need for help in Sarah's room. Marie responded to the now-vacant room and empty bed. She heard Sarah's spirit say, "I'm okay."

The call light blinked incessantly for two weeks, turning off and on of its own accord at different intervals during the day. The maintenance people spent the next two weeks trying to fix the blinking light, thinking it was an electrical short. Marie knew what was causing it—Sarah's spirit.

Just as Marie's angel dolls are able to transfer love and healing, it is also possible to send your physician guide to oversee an outcome for someone else. When Lillian's son John was gravely ill in the hospital, Lillian asked her doctor guide, Blue Moon, to attend John at his bedside to aid in his recovery. Apparently the guide's presence helped John, because he returned home soon after.

Sylvia DeLong has a particular physician in spirit whom she loans to those who need healing. He was a Harvard graduate when he was on the earth plane and he now works with a group of doctors from the spirit side of life. Just prior to the completion of this book, I had the good fortune to receive his attention while I was in the hospital for surgery. At Sylvia's direction, I began calling upon the doctor five days before my scheduled date for surgery. The very first time I called for him, I could feel his presence around me and felt that he was doing something with my body. Once in the hospital, I called upon him several more times, sort of as a reminder to look after me. The good doctor must have been true to his calling, because something certainly saved me from a near-fatal mishap.

While my husband sat next to my bed reading, I was blissfully sleeping after surgery, apparently "going to the light," unbeknownst to anyone. I had been given too much morphine for the diminutive size of my body and my breathing had slowed down to eight breaths a minute. It is my understanding that morphine slows down the breathing process, and that is exactly what it had done to me. A nurse happened into the room, discovered my situation, and quickly brought in another nurse to look at me. In no time there were four nurses hovering over me, shouting my name, according to my husband. I vaguely remember opening my eyes and closing them, and opening my eyes again, only to close them. Oprah Winfrey's talk show was on the television, and my husband, knowing that I adore Oprah, kept telling me that Oprah was on. I remember looking at the television screen and closing my eyes several times. This attempt to awaken me went on for awhile until I was more conscious. Needless to say, they took me off the morphine and replaced the pain medication with another formula. I give credit to the good doctor in spirit for maneuvering this calamity into a positive outcome. Also, I give gracious thanks to the nurses who came to my aid.

Marie's husband, Louis Gates, has two spirits who come to him when he is ill. The first is a young Indian maiden with long, black hair, who dresses in buckskin and wears a turquoise beaded necklace with an emblem in the center. She brings medicine in bowls and smelly potions that she shows to Louis. The other spirit is a gentleman who appears in a black suit and hat, carrying a black medical bag. The two guides work in tandem from the spirit side of life to bring healing to Louis. After they depart, Louis notices a difference in his condition.

Sylvia DeLong shared some interesting experiences with me about how spirits assist in health areas. She is keenly aware of receiving the benefits of Dr. Medford's and Dr. Randy's talents on numerous occasions. Dr. Medford was Dr. Randy's professor. He brought Dr. Medford to Sylvia saying, "This is the one you need," when she was having difficulties when her father was very ill and could not communicate well. Dr. Medford is a Scottish doctor and he helped Sylvia in many ways with her father's care, such as giving her physical strength to move him about.

When Sylvia's mother had a pacemaker implanted, Dr. Medford was the one who alerted Sylvia that her mother needed her. Sylvia was at home relaxing before visiting her mother at the hospital, anticipating her release the next day. Suddenly, she saw Dr. Medford sitting in a chair in his white coat, a slender man with red hair, and then the image faded. She had never seen him prior to this incident and hasn't since. Apparently it was so important that he get her attention, he manifested. Sylvia went into a meditative mode and received the message, "Go to the hospital now. She's being released." Sylvia immediately got into the car and drove to the hospital. Sure enough, Hilda was waiting for her in the lobby. She had forgotten how to use the telephone. Apparently Hilda's memory was slipping at that time and no one realized it. Sylvia was very grateful to spirit for alerting her.

Another interesting incident that Sylvia shared was when she developed an extremely high fever as a young girl, which she now suspects was rheumatic fever. Sylvia's fever kept raging, which caused her mother, Hilda, to be terribly worried. In those days one didn't run to doctors quickly. To make matters worse, Hilda could not find the thermometer to take Sylvia's temperature. That night Hilda had a vision. A large polar bear took Sylvia in his arms and drew her under the ice and then brought her back to the surface. The next morning the fever had broken and Sylvia was fine. Spirit later told Hilda that they hid the thermometer so she wouldn't be worried sick.

The average person may not find their physician guide to be as prominent as those people who work within the healing professions or are mediums. But guiding assistance is still available to you when questions of health arise. Each of us has the ability to "feel" an area of our body that needs attention. Through meditation we can communicate with our physician guide in order to receive information regarding what course of action to take when we develop a condition. The information received could range from starting to exercise, changing your diet, visiting an herbalist, or seeking out a medical doctor.

The Chemist

Physical phenomena was quite popular from the 1850s through the 1920s as a means to prove the continuity of life and the ability to communicate with the spirit world. It was the chemist guide who adjusted the medium's body to accommodate the physically exhausting channeling of spirit entities that were necessary to perform such phenomena as materialization of spirits and floating trumpets. Ectoplasm was necessary to produce the phenomena, and the chemist is the spirit who made the adjustment within the medium to produce it.

Phenomena is not practiced to much extent now, and the quality of what is presented today should be viewed with skepticism, in my opinion. However, in the days when the Rev. Dr. Warren Hoover was attending classes for mediumship, he witnessed some extraordinary and legitimate phenomena.

During séances, Warren has been privileged to see such marvelous happenings as the appearance of highly evolved spirits with differently colored jewels glowing on their foreheads. The jewels signified the different levels of their spiritual training. When the spirits were asked about the gemstones, they said they were their Stars of Progression. They gained these "stars" through the study of natural law and by helping people on earth. These spirits apparently sat at the feet of the "universal masters" in order to progress to higher levels of spirituality.

The chemist guide is not an active member of hardly anyone's band anymore since physical phenomena is not currently prevalent. Our body chemistry has changed so much due to the medicines prescribed for us, the chemically preserved food we eat, and the quality of our environment that our bodies are not conducive for the channeling of spirit phenomena to any extent.

The Teacher

The teacher guide is usually prominent in an individual's life when a person is a teacher by profession or when works with children in some other capacity, such as a daycare worker or physical therapist. I believe when they work with children on any level, we are automatically teaching.

Once when I was drawing a spirit guide for a client, I became aware that this guide had been a teacher in England during a previous life. I felt that he had come to America on the Mayflower and eventually established schools and universities on the East Coast. I conveyed this information to my client and told her that his position was that of a teacher guide. My client told me that she was a teacher by profession, and her family for generations had also been teachers. Not only that, she was a descendant of people who came over on the Mayflower.

A teacher guide's purpose may also be to aid an individual in responding appropriately to their karmic challenges. At times I will refer to this guide as a teacher of life, one who is present during experiences meant to bring growth to an individual. The teacher guide can be of the most assistance when we are experiencing situations that appear to be unfair. If we meditate on the circumstances that brought about the situation we find unjust, we may discover that we are experiencing a karmic balancing. In other words, we are experiencing the same thing we inflicted upon another previously. If we judged someone harshly, we are being judged. If we fired people with little or no cause, we are being fired for no sound reason. If we were involved in dishonest business practices, we might find ourselves on the other end of the stick, so to speak. What goes around, comes around.

These are valuable learning experiences, events given to us to advance our spiritual growth. Turn to your teacher in meditation the next time life appears unfair. What you learn should be enlightening.

The Philosopher

The next guide may also be referred to by the title doctor as well as philosopher. I like to tell people this is the Ph.D. (So we have an M.D. guide and a Ph.D. guide.) The philosopher's purpose is to bring guidance in material matters, such as managing a business, selling your home, buying stock, organizing a budget, or, on a lesser scale, balancing your checkbook. This guide's strongest influence can be readily seen in those individuals who are logical, grounded people. This guide most commonly makes its presence known during a session when I am doing a drawing for a man. Not that I am in any way implying that women aren't logical and grounded, but men who come for spirit guide drawings are usually more concerned with their professional lives than their spiritual ones, so I have found. Under those circumstances, it would be appropriate for the philosopher guide to make its presence known rather than a master teacher, for instance.

The philosopher works on a mental level and is instrumental in helping us understand our karmic lessons also. This spirit works hand-in-hand with the teacher guide to assist us in acquiring the attitudes and philosophies that are intended to lead us to our highest personal development. Through meditation, we are able to receive information from the philosopher.

While walking through the aisles in a bookstore, it isn't unheard of for the philosopher to call attention to a particular book that will assist in someone's higher development. Spirits choose such interesting ways to impress us with ideas. Some people have remarked to me how books have fallen to the floor, and when they were inspected, found to be just what they needed.

The Native

The American Indian seems to be the guide everyone is most familiar with and expects to receive when in a consultation with a medium. A more accurate title, though, would be native. The country a person is born in is their native country, and that is the nationality of their native guide. Since the American Indian is the true native of the United States, it is the Native American Indian that appears most often in this native position when I am drawing a guide for a client (since I live in the United States as do most of my clients).

There was a time in our history when the North American Indians were considered to be the masters of psychic laws and had a profound knowledge of what some people would call supernormal forces. When they made their transition to the spirit side of life, they carried these qualities with them. From spirit, the natives are the rulers of nature. They honor Mother Earth, the four seasons, the four directions, and feel a kinship to the elements of the earth.

Sylvia DeLong was told by her Native American guides how to talk to nature. When there is a thunderstorm, Sylvia goes outside and speaks to the storm, saying, "Brother storm, you are most welcome, but please, no tree limbs, no damage to this house. Please, no lightning, but you are welcome." One female Indian spirit told the DeLong family that if they wanted a bough for a bed, to ask the tree if they may have her bough. She expressed that it was always important to show respect to nature.

The Indian guide, or native, is also a protector. Many people feel the presence of their Indian guides sitting next to them in a car when they travel, and some tell stories about accidents being averted due to their Indian guides. One such story came from Diane Davis. She told me about an impression she received some years ago when she was driving home from Gainesville, Florida, on a dark road after teaching a natural law class. Diane had the impression of an Indian frantically hanging onto the roof of the car, being thrown from side to side as she drove the posted fifty-five mile-an-hour speed limit. She immediately removed her foot from the accelerator and waited for something to happen, not knowing what to expect. Within seconds her headlights shone on a huge deer standing in the middle of the road. Because she had slowed the speed of the car, she was easily able to drive around the animal and return safely home.

The Rev. Lillian Weigl also feels protection from one Indian spirit, in particular, during her readings. Apparently he is a very tall man who first appeared to her when she lived in Winter Park, Florida, and he would stare out the window in her office. The Indian only came when strange men were present for a reading, as if to indicate that should she need protection, he was there. He did not appear to her for many years until just recently, when he presented himself in her home in Cassadaga. She does not know his name or anything about him, only recognizing the protection he extends to her.

Many people in recent years have become fascinated by the Indian culture, I believe, showing the influence of the spirit world upon us and being an indication that society is opening up to the guiding forces of spirit helpers.

The Joy Guide

Children are impish and mischievous as a rule. The joy guide most often appears as a child, and they, too, can display behavior that would be described as mischievous. I refer to this guide as the practical joker at work within all of us, the one who is responsible for bringing out the lighter side of our personalities. When mirth and merriment manifest within a group of people unexpectedly for no particular reason, it is frequently the presence of someone's joy guide causing the frivolity.

Many years ago, whenever a friend of mine would have a gathering at her house, her cousin in spirit would invariably be present to add sparkle to the occasion. People who were usually somber would brighten their attitude. Spontaneous laughter was commonplace with even the most serious attendees. Normal situations became comedic.

This particular guide is usually not a dominant figure in the band, unless you happen to be a comedian or clown by profession. Normally, the only time this guide will present itself to me during a consultation is as a signal that my client needs to be lifted out of a negative attitude and seek some fun. I tell my client they need to go play.

In our "get ahead" society, perhaps we should pay more attention to this guide. We could all certainly benefit from less stress by viewing some matters with a sense of humor. Call upon your joy guide when your daily life becomes overwhelming. Ask to be shown the humor in the situation. Whatever is occurring at the time, you can always ask to view things differently.

The Master Teacher

This is a very special guide. The master teacher imparts to us spiritual wisdom and philosophy, frequently that of the Far East. They may appear as a Hindu, a Buddhist monk, an Asian, or someone representative of India. For a person studying a spiritual path, this guide is of great importance. The Far Eastern culture has many lessons to share with a student. Marie Lilla's master teacher is a tall, slender gentleman who appears to be in his fifties. She feels he is quite possibly a Hindu and dresses in a white robe. He assists Marie when she is giving readings.

Should the average person not aspire to become a minister or work in some capacity within the spiritual or metaphysical world, the guidance he or she receives from the master teacher would help him or her to acquire a more spiritual perception of life in general. People who are social activists or devote time to fighting against animal cruelty and other humane causes certainly are strongly influenced by their master teachers.

My husband and I were fortunate to happen upon a group of people demonstrating in a park during the Christmas holidays of 1991. The park is famous for attracting demonstrators because it is located directly across from the White House in Washington, D.C. People had gathered in Lafayette Park on Christmas Eve for the purpose of lifting the consciousness of the nation to the plight of the homeless. The main speaker and organizer was the Rev. Jesse Jackson. It was an electrifying experience. The sound of brass horns thrilled our spines and rhapsodic voices sang out to moving gospel music. I will never forget chanting with the crowd the phrase, "Keep hope alive. All God's children, keep hope alive!" It was the best Christmas Eve of my life, thus far. At the end of the presentation, I actually stood above the Rev. Jackson as he lay on the ground in his sleeping bag, intentionally violating the law by this action.

After experiencing the Rev. Jackson's vibrant energy, I would have to feel that he is strongly motivated by his master teacher. However, since he is a minister of the Baptist faith, I doubt he recognizes this influence and would not agree with me.

When Miko, my master teacher, is present, I am aware of the smell of incense. She is Asian, which certainly accounts for my attraction to the Orient. Her black hair frames a pretty, smiling face. Usually she appears wearing a red kimono, but also shows herself in normal street clothes that you or I would wear.

I believe Miko first came to me when I was nineteen and had become great friends with a Japanese woman who worked with me at a department store in the suburbs of Washington, D.C. Judy and I worked part-time at the jewelry counter: she, supplementing her income, and me, earning spending money during my senior year in high school. Judy taught me how to use chopsticks and introduced me to all kinds of Asian food, including sushi, tempura, and sashimi. During that time I also developed a taste for Asian-style furnishings. Throughout our friendship, Judy and I comforted each other through some difficult experiences and supported one another emotionally for a number of years, until we lost touch after I moved to Ohio. The reason I feel my master teacher came to me at that time is because of the impact Judy had on my life. In later years I learned that it is common to experience a synchronicity of events. When one suddenly becomes attracted to a culture or hobby, for instance, spirit is usually the guiding force behind the attraction.

The Creator Guide

This guide is instrumental in bringing inspiration to artists, authors, and musicians. The creator guide helps us manifest the talents and gifts we have been blessed with, be they dancing, singing, or crafts. We call on this guide for the missing lyric in our composition, the phrase that will release the writer's block, the appropriate step in the choreography we are perfecting.

I once had an artist friend who created beautiful works through the use of fabric. He would sit at his sewing machine and allow his hands to be guided by spirit wherever they were led, creating unique designs. When he felt the sewing process was complete, he would view the pattern stitched on the fabric and apply paint in the areas he felt were appropriate. He said he never ceased to be amazed by the outcome.

Another artist friend of mine worked in tapestry. Most of her work was sold to churches, since the tapestries depicted the Disciples. As she created, she told me she felt the presence of the religious figures. I have to say, her work was extraordinary.

Regarding the composition of the song *Yesterday*, Paul McCartney has said that he could not explain how it was created. He felt he sort of dreamed it, and when he awoke, it was just there. Many musicians, I feel, are guided by the higher side of life, whether they recognize this influence or not. How else can we explain the unexplainable? Where does the melody and lyrics flow from? I believe spirit channels the information to us from God.

Sometimes we are able to control inspiration, and other times it is like a random attack out of nowhere. During the times when I make an attempt to control inspiration, I sit in meditation to receive what I need. Afterward I either make a journal entry detailing the information or sit at the computer reworking passages in my newest book until I receive what I am intended to have.

As to random attacks of inspiration, there was a period in my life when I was creating a lot of oil paintings. Spirit would bring flashes of inspiration to me as I drove down the street in my car. Rock-and-roll music would blast from the radio, which is not supposed to be a conducive environment in which to receive inspiration, but regardless, I would suddenly become aware of an image in the clouds or trees. Sometimes flashes of color would pop into my head. The latter would usually happen when I knew the image I wanted to paint, but had not received the inspiration for the colors I would use.

Creator teachers are fascinating to work with. They have such unique ways of bringing inspiration to us. My creator teacher is named Michael. He wears his brown hair in a bowl cut and has a full beard and twinkly blue eyes. Michael says that he was an artist when he was on the earth plane. Judging from his attire, I would say he lived during the 1400s.

Domestic Helpers

Many people give credit to spirits for assisting with domestic chores. Sylvia DeLong speaks with high regard about a lady who came to her cooking aid. You see, Sylvia never cooked until after her mother, Hilda, had to go into a nursing home. Apparently cooking was her mother's task when they were living together. When Sylvia was faced with having to cook for herself, Dr. Medford and Dr. Randy brought a spirit to Sylvia's rescue. Her name was Mary, a very sweet Scottish lady. Mary would impress her with recipes, along with specific ingredients and detailed instructions. These were recipes that Sylvia herself would never have been able to create without the assistance of this spirit lady.

Sylvia doesn't eat much meat, but Mary kept insisting that she would enjoy this particular stew. Mary told her, "You're going to like it." So Sylvia made the recipe. (For the actual recipe, see Appendix One.)

Universal Masters

Universal masters are highly evolved entities who have fulfilled their karma through many incarnations on the earth plane and have continued to evolve on the spirit side to become the enlightened beings they are. Their duty is to assist all of us spiritually, whether we are a spirit embodied within the human form or a spirit who has made the transition to the other side of life. All of us may call upon any of the universal masters when we feel the need for their services. Examples of such universal masters would be St. Germain, Jesus, Sophia, Buddha, Krishna, and Mary. Seeking the assistance of a universal master would be similar to a person of the Catholic faith praying to one of the saints for guidance.

When seeking the comfort of these enlightened beings, I would not encourage anyone to anticipate a full manifestation of a universal master to occur within their bedroom or wherever it is that meditation is practiced. However, I would anticipate that you should feel an affirming sensation and have the feeling of well-being and peace afterward.

Guardian Angels

This seems to be the appropriate place to address the question of whether a guardian angel is the same as or similar to a spirit guide. Angels are spiritual beings who are in a class all by themselves. What makes them angelic is that they have never incarnated on the earth plane, unlike our spirit teachers. Their affiliation is with the elemental kingdom—in other words, nature spirits, those special beings we know by the titles of gnomes, fairies, salamanders, sylphs, water sprites, and elves. The nature kingdom lives in a parallel existence to ours, and they evolve in their plane as we do in ours. When the nature spirits evolve from the above-titled states of being, they exist in an angelic form. Some progress to become guardian angels. Our personal guardian angel is with us from birth until we make our transition. So is the gatekeeper, but they are not the same. One has not lived in human form while the other has.

As humans, we are fortunate to have so many means in which to draw support. Not only do we have spirit teachers, friends, relatives, and loved ones who are interested and devoted to our highest and best development, we also have the angelic kingdom.

Many wonderful and enlightening books have been written on the subject of angels, and I would encourage anyone who thirsts for more information regarding angels to peruse the local bookseller's shelves.

SIX

DISCERNING SPIRIT

W hen we attempt to discern spirit, it is very easy to mistake one guide for another if we are judging by appearance alone. During meditation, should you happen to see an Asian face or an American Indian in full headdress, do not assume that this is your master teacher or native guide. The Asian face could be that of a former Chinese herbalist who now performs as your physician guide. The American Indian could very well be your gatekeeper, since he was a leader among his people when he was on the earth plane, for instance.

It is possible to have three American Indians in your band, as an example, or perhaps two Asians. The Rev. Lillian Weigl has, besides her protective native guide, two other American Indians. One is named Hanna. She wears black shoes with buttons up the side and a long calico dress. Hanna comes to Lillian only when there is a disturbance or problem concerning children. Approximately one week after Hanna introduced herself to Lillian, a lady came for a reading. She was so sad. When the lady sat down, Hanna appeared at Lillian's side with three children sitting around her. All the children were dripping with water. Lillian asked the women how many children she had and she answered three. Lillian said, "Yes, and you lost them in a drowning accident." The women let out a shriek. "Wait," said Lillian, "they are in the care of an American Indian named Hanna, and they will always be cared for." This revelation was a great comfort to the woman.

Cinderella is the name Lillian gave to her third American Indian guide, until one day a gentleman created a drawing of the guide in charcoal and called her Blue Moon. Lillian asked how he knew that was her name. He told her simply, "She told me so." Blue Moon is a healer, and her exact likeness hangs on Lillian's wall today. She appears to be an attractive woman in her twenties with pigtails.

Through meditation you will be able to discern who your guides are and how they assist in your life. To establish whether or not you are actually contacting a personal guide, you will have to test the spirit. This can be an exercise in trial and error while you are building a communication with your higher guidance. Constant fine-tuning may be necessary. One day your guide may come into your meditation easily and then the next time you "sit in the silence" (meditation), absolutely nothing happens. Remember that you are raising your vibrations at the same time that your guides are lowering theirs. Sometimes the two vibrations may not mesh correctly.

I would suggest that when you feel a successful communication has been established that you ask for guidance in an immediate situation. An issue that is currently involving your job would be an excellent place to begin. During meditation, ask questions of your guide. Speak to the guide as you would a best friend, except do so in your head, not aloud. A true guide would not give an answer that is contrary to your character or suggest revenge. Apply the answers you receive and wait for the results. If everything goes wrong by following the guidance given, you may be misinterpreting what you are receiving, or the spirit may not be a true guide of yours. Patience and dedication will prove whether or not you are communicating with a true guide or a mischievous spirit.

The Rev. Dr. Warren Hoover suggests that if you have been attempting to receive from a spirit and nothing is happening, you need to ask for another spirit teacher. Even when we have worked with a guide for a number of years, it is permissible to ask for a replacement when there seems to be a standstill in the communication.

If Napoleon, Cleopatra, Elvis, or some other famous personality should manifest during meditation, either as a spirit passing through or declares they are your personal guide, please consider the likelihood of this carefully. There are two trains of thought here to consider. First, it is possible that when someone envisions Ben Franklin or any other noted figure as his or her spirit guide, he or she is drawing from his or her memory bank of historical personalities or allowing his or her ego to interpret an impersonation by a naughty, mischievous spirit as being a reality. On the other hand, why couldn't Elvis have an interest in a particularly talented guitarist on the earth plane and feel drawn to share his musical expertise with this guitarist? You are the only one who is in the position to make the determination of who is a true guide if a famous personality manifests. However, do exercise all the possibilities before leaping to a conclusion.

Occasionally people who have had a very orthodox religious upbringing will believe that Jesus is their personal guide. There are two sides to that coin. Master teachers frequently resemble what society envisions Jesus' appearance to be, so one could easily mistake a master teacher for Christ. Sometimes this assumption can be a reaction due to a departure from established Christian religious beliefs learned as a child and the embracing of the more esoteric—New Age, if you will—philosophies in adult years. When one seeks to learn about Eastern religions and nonorthodox teachings, they soon discover that there are many paths to "heaven." This can be disconcerting to someone who has been taught all of their life traditional Christian beliefs. But as a person becomes more familiar and comfortable with the alternative philosophies (and discovers that God isn't going to strike them dead for practicing these teachings), they may not respond in this manner in the future. It is easy to understand how our conditioning can influence our reality when we are exposed to other alternatives. Sometimes it just takes time to adjust.

Because of her heavy German Lutheran background, the Rev. Lillian Weigl has often stated that the first time she declared she was a Spiritualist, she waited for a bolt of lightning to strike her down. Of course, that never happened.

Now, the other side of the coin. Jesus is for anyone who seeks his comfort, as is Buddha, Krishna, Mary, or St. Germain. They are, after all, universal masters, highly evolved spirits. We can always call upon Jesus, any other religious figure, or a saint with affirmations and prayers when we are in need. And if we feel that Jesus paid us a private visit at some low point in our lives, then that is our reality. I know of several mediums who feel Christ came to them during a time of great difficulty. This seems to be especially true in cases where healing was needed. Again, you are the only one who can make this determination about Jesus or any other prominent religious figure who comes to visit.

The image of the Virgin Mary mysteriously formed on the windows of a building just north of St. Petersburg, Florida, in 1994. People were attracted to the amazing sight to such a degree that candles and flowers adorn, even today, make-shift shrines along with pictures and letters taped to the wall. Tests were conducted by the company that installed the windows and determined that the cause of the manifestation was in the glass and not a chemical reaction from cleaning fluids. The photo is courtesy of Richard Bengtson, a reiki master living in Florida.

Given that universal masters are so highly evolved, it is entirely within the realm of possibility that someone of the Virgin Mary's status, for instance, could manifest to people. We have all heard of appearances of this nature around the world. Many skeptics pooh-pooh this notion, though. Dr. Hoover believes that an entity of this high evolvement could appear, but why would they? He feels it would have to be due to a very high magnitude of importance. Averting World War III would fall under that category, he says.

Other mediums believe that an appearance by Mary may simply be for the purpose of giving people hope, especially those who live in impoverished countries. And then again, what about the commuters passing by the building located just north of St. Petersburg, Florida, where an image of Mary appeared daily on a window? (See opposite page for photo and story.) Perhaps it was intended to uplift the commuters' spirits as they traveled to work. June Schmitt, a well-known healer and medium in Cassadaga, believes that Mary's appearances were to encourage people to return to spirituality. I look at it this way: If it makes you happy to believe that universal masters can draw so close to us and manifest in such public ways, so be it. As long as this belief hurts no one, it cannot be harmful.

What do you do when you have discerned that a naughty spirit is impersonating a famous personality? If you have determined that a little culprit is trying to tempt your ego, refuse to give it any attention and send the spirit into the white light. Here is how to accomplish that.

While in meditation, visualize a brilliant white light, the whitest white you can imagine. See it in whatever form you choose, such as a white candle flame or a ball of vibrant white light. With your mind, push the spirit into the light. If you cannot exactly see the spirit, visualize it as a round chunk, a nondescript form of gray matter, a blob. See the chunk go into the white light. Mentally you might want to encourage the process by saying, "Into the light, go into the light." Once the spirit is in the light, it will be cleansed and taken to where it will be given the assistance it needs to evolve. If you feel so inclined, mentally say a prayer for the spirit's highest and best interests to be brought forward now. Then visualize the white light ascending away from you until you cannot see it anymore.

Some people have expressed to me a concern that a guide may not be looking out for their best interests or even have some ill intent. A guide's purpose is to lead, direct, and show the way for our highest and best good. Hence, the word guide. The title has positive connotations. Remember, spirit teachers are emissaries of good. Their intentions are honorable and positive. If a person has established communication with a true guide, he or she will be led only to his or her highest and best good. Most mediums will tell you that when they are around their spirit energy, they feel uplifted, that it is a peaceful and joyous experience. After all, the energy comes from God.

Always remember that you are in control. Interference from a naughty spirit is coming from another plane of existence. It cannot do anything unless you give the spirit power by thinking that it has control. Even personal spirit guides do not have total control. They only exert influence. I have often heard it said that we have more to fear from our human encounters than those from spirit.

Oftentimes, spirits who appear to be naughty are simply attempting to be funny. Sometimes the result is more annoying than funny, but we should give them credit anyway for displaying a sense of humor. The following is a story Fran Ellison told me regarding a mischievous spirit who lived in a home she once owned in New Smyrna Beach, Florida.

Fran had purchased a bag of onions from the store. After returning home, she placed them where she always stored her onions, planning to use some of the onions to make potato salad for a camping trip she and her boyfriend had arranged. After her boyfriend had gone ahead to the campground, Fran started to prepare the salad. When she was ready to chop the onions, she discovered the bag had disappeared. She searched everywhere but could not locate the onions.

Fran was forced to return to the store to purchase another bag of onions. She was furious with her boyfriend, figuring he had taken the onions with him to the campground. After she finally was able to make the potato salad, Fran placed the remaining onions in the bag in the normal storage area. She proceeded to the campground and gave her boyfriend heck for taking the onions. He denied having anything to do with her disappearing onions. When they returned from the camping trip a couple of days later, much to Fran's surprise, there were two bags of onions located in the storage area. No one else had access to the house while she was away.

Fran said that many such incidents occurred in that particular house over the years. She knows it was the mischievous spirit living there that caused the upsets from time to time.

It is a natural law that like attracts like. When I was growing up, I remember my mother always saying, "Birds of a feather flock together." The same principle applies with spirit teachers. Your vibration will draw guiding forces that are similar to you. The DeLong family attracted spirit people who were predominantly from Scotland and England, which was their heritage.

Early in the relationship that Lillian Weigl formed with her guide Jerry, he told her, "You're going to learn that I like the youngin's (children) and I love the pretty ladies." Lillian said that Jerry fit right in with her family. Her father and son both liked the ladies and she loved children.

We must remember that our earthly companions have a great influence on our lives, too. Sometimes we are even judged by the company we keep, fairly or unfairly. It is Sylvia DeLong's opinion that we should seek the company of saints. In order to receive the highest guidance, I personally feel it is a good idea to be the best person you are capable of being at this time in your life and to choose good companions, those from whose elbows will rub off spiritual qualities.

The more ethical, honest, and positive a person you are, the higher the vibration you will attract. Of course, none of us are true saints, and I am not suggesting that we must behave as such in order to attract good spirits. We just need to be the best we can. One method is to practice "positive action." The Rev. Jerry Frederich feels that we need to keep some sort of positive action in motion; in other words, somehow we must seek to improve life, be it animal, person, or plant. This works for him. If he steps away from this positive action, chaos breaks out in his life.

If you think meditation and spirit communication is a game, you best think again. During meditation we attract more than spirit guides, as I have stated. Meditation has often been likened to a light bulb. When we meditate, a light is sent out into the universe and spirits see the light and are drawn to it. Therefore, you will attract spirits besides your guides who are of like mind and disposition also. If you are negative in your thinking and actions, some of the spirits you attract could be similar, and influence you in a manner that would not be beneficial to your spiritual growth and overall well being. Meditation is not a game, and spirit communication should not be taken casually.

Sylvia DeLong sometimes feels spirits that we encounter are earthbound, frustrated, perhaps misguided, and have not gone to the light. The DeLong family had an experience with a woman's spirit that would match this description. After moving into their home in Cassadaga, a woman dressed in white would appear occasionally to Sylvia and her father. Each began to notice something dark in the den area of their home at this time. Then Sylvia's mother, who was especially sensitive to picking up people's moods, became a "holy terror" after being in the den, having fits of depression and anger afterward.

A well-known medium by the name of Billy Hammond came to visit and picked up the presence of this woman's spirit, telling them that a woman dressed in white used to live there and that she was troubled. Later, during a group meditation, the family's guiding forces came through to say that there was a spirit in the house who thinks she still lives there. She was a very unhappy woman and is now an unhappy spirit. They instructed the family to turn the lights on in the den and open the windows. That relieved the house of the presence of this unhappy woman in spirit.

The activities we participate in are also arenas for attracting spirits of similar character. Spirits can be attracted to us when we frequent places where spirits inhabit, and I am not speaking about your local haunted house. Spirits are everywhere. If a spirit had been an avid tennis player while on the earth plane, it is possible to attract this entity when attending a tennis match or playing tennis. The same would hold true regarding socializing in bars. Spirits who congregate in bars enjoyed alcohol when they were on the earth plane. Each spirit mentioned has a desire to associate with a person who either plays tennis or drinks so they can vicariously experience the "thrill" they received when on earth. Of course, it is also true that a former alcoholic who has become enlightened on the spirit side of life could be drawn to a person specifically so they may assist in that person's recovery from an addiction.

We need to recognize that these are possibilities we open ourselves up to when we seek to contact spirit. My statements are not intended to make anyone uncomfortable, merely to make you aware that spirits simply want to be recognized. When we meditate and spirits see the lights we are sending out, they want to come into our energy fields. When spirits have recently crossed over or have not evolved to any extent from their earthly behaviors, they may attempt communication with whoever meditates and is of like mind. Like attracts like.

I have not had the experience of attracting a lot of spirits with negative personalities when I meditate. When I am giving a reading or meditating, I am not barraged by unhappy, addictive spirits either. I believe that it is wise to choose to not identify with the concept that some spirits are not of the highest and best. In life, the very thing we fear or give attention to frequently is exactly what we attract to us. For instance, someone worries over losing his or her job, so he or she spends time creating that scenario in his or her mind instead of contemplating how he or she can improve his or her performance. So, don't own the idea of anything but positive spirits. Anticipate positive and you will attract positive.

Naughty is not evil. Children are naughty, but they aren't evil. But even naughty spirits do not, as a rule, come into my energy field. Am I a perfect person? No. Am I a teetotaler? No. Neither am I a negative person. I am a spirit experiencing life in a human vehicle, just like you. I do the best I can with the experience I have attained at this time. I attract nice spirits. So can you.

The Rev. Dr. Warren Hoover has never seen an evil spirit either. He also has quite a history with the investigation of haunted houses. Even under those circumstances, Warren has not come across evil entities.

Diane Davis believes that there are forces with intentions that are not ethically her own. Because of that, those intentions can look drastically different. She does not look upon certain spirits as being evil or bad because that is a polarity she believes we have been taught. Just like there are personalities in people she would not invite home to dinner, there are those intelligences in spirit that are of that same intent or quality.

If we strive to live our lives in a manner that will help us in our spiritual growth, we are not likely to attract lower entities. However, should we encounter a spirit that is undesirable (and haven't we all run across some undesirable human beings?), it is important to remember that we are the stronger ones. We are in control.

If you happen upon a negative spirit, say a prayer to bless the entity so that it aspires to evolve to a higher level of consciousness. Go through the process I outlined previously of sending the spirit into the white light. Not only will you rid yourself of the negative energy, you will be helping the spirit to grow. And that's a nice thing to do.

SEVEN

FIRST
AWARENESS

I thought you would find it interesting to read about how the mediums mentioned in this book first became aware of the spirit side of life and how they continued in their development. Each has a unique story to tell. Perhaps their experiences will mirror yours or trigger a memory that will enlighten you.

Lillian Weigl felt she was different when growing up. She saw auras during her early years at school. Once she commented to her friends about the beauty of a blue coat with a fox collar that a woman was wearing. Her playmates thought she was crazy and promptly told all the children at school that Lillian couldn't distinguish between the color of green and blue. What the children had seen was a lady dressed in a green coat. But Lillian had seen the blue aura of the woman, which overshadowed the color of the coat. After that experience, Lillian was more cautious about what she said to people when she saw auras.

As an adult, Lillian's life took many twists and turns. She became a widow at an early age with a son to raise. Her interests at that time were on a more mundane level than spiritual. One night a gentleman approached her in a restaurant for the purpose of giving her a psychic message. He correctly predicted that she would live in a religious community. Lillian thought at the time, why on earth would I ever do such a thing? It wasn't until her middle-age years that she began to study Spiritualism. At that time her psychic abilities from childhood were reawakened, and her awareness of spirit became stronger. She received most of her training from a now-defunct Spiritualist church in Orlando, Florida.

Arlene Sikora's first awareness of spirit was when she was six years old. Her grandmother had just passed to spirit and everyone was crying during the wake at the house. But Arlene couldn't understand why everyone was so upset. She could clearly see her grandmother standing on the staircase. When Arlene brought this to someone's attention, she was given no explanation. Almost every night for a year thereafter, her grandmother would pay her a visit, standing at the foot of Arlene's bed. This frightened Arlene, as it would any normal child. She ran to her parents to tell them about the visitations, but they could not explain these events. Eventually her parents became tired of this behavior, so Arlene denied her reality, and the grandmother's spirit did not return for several years.

When she was eleven years old, Arlene's family moved to Florida. The grandmother started appearing again, this time over the top of Arlene's bed enclosed within a cloud, which she now knows was ectoplasm. The grandmother's hand would come through the cloud, reaching toward her, and she would call to Arlene, which really terrified her. Again, Arlene told her parents what was happening. They still could not offer an explanation, so, once again, Arlene denied her reality to keep her sanity and that of the family.

When Arlene was twenty-eight years of age, she and her fiancé drove from Massachusetts, where she was living at the time, to Florida, for a vacation at Arlene's mother's home. While there she discovered a book in her mother's bedroom written by Jean Dixon called *Gift of Prophecy*. This both shocked and annoyed Arlene. All of Arlene's life her mother had stated that there was no truth in anything that was described within the pages of this book and, besides, being Catholic meant you didn't believe in such things. But

Jean Dixon was Catholic and had visions, and it was okay for her. Arlene's curiosity was aroused and her unexplained childhood memories came flooding back to her. During the trip back to Massachusetts, Arlene's fiancé announced that this was all nonsense and chastised her for considering that there was any validity to the unseen. His attitude only increased Arlene's desire to begin an exploration into the unknown, so she promptly ended the engagement.

Later in the year Arlene drove to Buffalo, New York, to pick up her godmother to drive her back to Massachusetts for a visit. Arlene was informed by members of the family about the Tupperware parties that her godmother was attending once a week. As it turned out, she was actually going to séances and meditation classes. On the ride back to Massachusetts, the godmother told Arlene all about the classes and her experiences. It was a life-changing ride. A trusted member of the family gave Arlene a realization about what she had experienced as a child, and it became a reality. Now she could understand and begin to develop her natural spiritual gifts to their full capacity.

Arlene began her training at Spiritualist churches in Massachusetts and eventually became a well-respected medium, teacher, healer, and minister with the National Spiritualist Association of Churches, which is the largest Spiritualist organization in the United States.

When Steve Hermann was three years old, he spoke to a grandfather he had never met in a dream. However, at that age, he thought he was speaking to God. It wasn't until eighteen years later, when Steve received a reading from a medium, that he was able to determine that it had been his grandfather he had spoken to in spirit at that young age. The medium had described the same image that Steve had seen in the dream. From that point he began his spiritual development in Spiritualist churches in the North. He, too, is affiliated with the National Spiritualist Association of Churches.

When Louis' great-grandfather, Chief Joseph, passed away, he came to sit on the edge of Louis' bed when he was three years old. After that, Louis saw spirits continually. Louis' mother, who was one-half Seneca Indian and a reader, taught him how to communicate with the spirit world. However, after Louis' parents divorced, his father forbid Louis to tell people what he could see on the spirit side of life. These were not pleasant times for Louis. His stepmother frequently voiced the opinion that he needed to be exorcised. But his spirit companions sustained him during his childhood circumstances, eventually leading him to Cassadaga in the 1990s. Louis quickly impressed the local mediums with his natural talent and proceeded to earn his certificate of mediumship in the next few years.

Diane recognizes that she possessed a strong intuitive ability beginning around the age of six. It wasn't something Diane could have consciously defined or labeled as a moment of intuition, but rather a knowingness that was pronounced, followed by a synchronistic event. One such incident was when she was visiting the Heard Museum in Phoenix, Arizona. The museum was conducting a cake walk for the children in the carnival area, so Diane lined up with the other children to participate. She looked over to see a lot of cakes and when she spied the chocolate one, Diane simply knew she was going to win it. And she did.

Diane began meditation classes in Cassadaga in 1972 for the purpose of self-growth and personal improvement. She did not have a preconceived idea that she could do anything nor an expectation of what might even happen in classes. However, Diane was quickly classified as a natural intuitive and within six months of attending classes, she was discerning spirit. While still a student and prior to her ordination, Diane was capable of delivering three-minute evidential messages (messages that give evidence to their accuracy) to fifty people, which would have taxed an experienced medium.

When Marie Lilla was a little girl, she used to tell her mother things that later would come true. One example was when she saw a man walking in their neighborhood and told her mother, "That man is sick. He needs help." Then the next day the gentleman had a heart attack. Marie explains her youthful psychic abilities as simply a "knowing," and took the gift for granted, feeling that it was a normal way to function in life.

At the age of twelve, when her father passed away, Marie immediately started to talk to him. She would ask him to wake her up in the morning, help her with an exam, and when she had any problems, she would say, "Come on down, I need your help." Something would always happen to assist her in the problem area.

After awhile she wondered if this was a normal thing to be doing. Maybe it was her imagination. So Marie asked her father, "Is this my imagination? If it is, fine, but if not, give me a sign. I want to know." Within an hour Marie received a definite sign that her father was communicating with her. The sign was so special that her father said it was to be kept between him and her and not to be disclosed.

In the 1960s, Marie traveled from Orlando to Cassadaga to attend weekly natural law classes with Eloise Page. She later began cultivating her natural mediumistic abilities in development circles in Cassadaga in the early 1980s. Marie earned her credentials as a certified medium and ordained minister and moved to Cassadaga from the hustle and bustle of Orlando.

When Patti Aubrey was five years old, her sensitivities were awakened. A huge image of Jesus' face flashed on the wall of her bedroom in white and gold. Considering her young age, Patti was unable to understand the reason for this manifestation. Since Patti also remembers being able to hear and sense spirit during her childhood, and recalls at night seeing angels shooting across the sky like stars, it is likely she received a special blessing from the manifestation of Jesus. As a young girl Patti just knew things. But her parents, like many parents often do, unfortunately told her she was weird.

When Patti was a mature adult, she came to Cassadaga for a reading with Kenneth Custance in the early 1980s. She was quite shaken by the experience. Kenneth told her things that her mother in spirit wanted conveyed to Patti. While the accuracy of the reading totally shocked her, something seemed familiar. Everything sort of meshed with her early childhood experiences.

Patti began classes shortly thereafter and was certified and ordained in Cassadaga some years later.

The Rev. Jerry Frederich was ten years old when he experienced a dramatic vision. Around 4 A.M., while still in a sleep state, Jerry saw a beautiful golden orchid. He remembers feeling the presence of angels, although he could not see them, hearing the most beautiful music he has ever heard in his life and angel voices singing. Jerry was impressed with the magnificent brightness of the light and carried the sensation and memory of this experience with him for at least four hours afterward.

Jerry recognized this manifestation to be of a high spiritual nature, so his interpretation, given his exposure to spiritual things at that time, was that it was the second coming of Christ. By using the term "second coming," Jerry is referring to Christ being back on earth, not in judgment, but rather to say, "A job well done," or "Let's do something different." The vision was not meant to be interpreted as the end of the world, but rather a message of love and blessings. Looking back now, he feels he was realizing his own soul. While Jerry was in awe of this event, he also felt it was normal. Six months later, to the day, the exact same vision appeared again, right down to the same time in the morning. Interestingly, he had no other visions than these two.

When Jerry was around fourteen, he vividly remembers astral traveling. It began after he had seen a newsreel about the Australian bullroar (also seen in the movie *Crocodile Dundee*). The bullroar is an instrument crafted from rawhide and stones that is waved around by the shamans, producing a roaring sound. Bullroars were used to place a shaman in a different spiritual state.

Three or four weeks after the newsreel, Jerry was walking around in his uncle's woods, near a dirt road and a swamp. He found several slats from an orange crate, approximately two inches wide and four to five inches long. Jerry picked up one of the slats and threw it up in the air, as boys will do. When the slat came down, it turned on its side, rotating its way back to the ground. In doing so, it made the exact sound of the bullroars from Australia. Jerry repeated this exercise about four times when, suddenly, he was up in the trees looking down at himself flinging the slats up into the air. Jerry had astral-projected into the tree. He does not remember coming back into his body after this experience.

Jerry returned to the woods for three days to continue this activity. The third time he participated in this flinging motion with the slats and viewing himself from above, he decided to attempt something that involved movement. The thought occurred to Jerry to pay a visit to some girls he went to school with, who lived probably thirty miles away. He vividly remembers floating over the Chippewa River in Wisconsin, hovering approximately seventy-five feet above the body of water. Eventually he saw the girls feeding the chickens and doing other farming tasks. Jerry blanks out at this point as to what followed. He remembers becoming conscious around 8:30 that night, five hours after his astral-projection adventure began. Apparently he had eaten dinner with the family and assisted his uncle with the milking of the cows, yet had no memory of any of this.

After three days of astral projection, a voice told Jerry that if he continued to participate in this fashion, he would get into trouble. Jerry didn't astral travel again until he was in his thirties, when he purposely initiated another event without difficulty.

Some years later, amidst a breakup in a relationship, Jerry came to Cassadaga for a mini-reading. At that time he heard about natural law classes and began attending them, which led him to participate in development classes. Eventually Jerry was certified as a medium and ordained as a Spiritualist minister.

My first realization of spirit was when I was twenty-two and living over a very old restaurant in Martinsburg, West Virginia. One night I awoke to see a young woman dressed in white standing in the doorway. She had shoulder-length blond hair and was attractive, yet the sight of her scared me terribly, so I rolled over in my bed to face the opposite wall. I remember being afraid to turn back over for fear she would still be there. When I finally summoned up my courage to turn over, she was gone. Later that day I asked the owners of the restaurant if anyone had ever lived in that apartment fitting her description. The answer was no. I was never able to find out who she was or why she chose to visit me.

I developed an interest in astrology and candle burning following that spirit visitation. It wasn't too long afterward that Don and I were married, and as I mentioned previously, through him I learned that spirit communication was a possibility. It wasn't until I moved to Orlando, Florida, in 1978, that my spiritual journey really began to unfold.

After my divorce, I was interested in receiving a reading, so friends directed me to a medium named Ruth Callin. I found the whole experience so intriguing that I decided to attend development classes under her tutelage. Shortly after beginning classes, I foresaw in meditation a predictive message, unbeknownst to me. The images that were given to me were that of a woman in a hospital bed in pain and then a white coffin in a dark room. Inside the coffin was a woman dressed in white, and surrounding the casket were burning white candles. The next image was of a man dressed in a black hooded cloak. Two days later I was the woman in pain in the hospital bed due to an auto accident.

I had been a passenger in a vehicle driven by my boyfriend at the time. We didn't wear seatbelts in those days, so I was thrown to the floor after crashing into the dashboard several times. My life totally changed from that moment on. The boyfriend dropped me, friends disappeared, except for one, and my activities were limited while I healed from numerous injuries and later began therapy for my injured knee. It was a terrible time in my life and I became quite depressed. My roommate was attending classes for meditation in Cassadaga, so she suggested that I join her, and I did.

The medium whose class I attended told me that my soul had been given a choice to continue to live on the earth plane or cross over into spirit. The image I had seen of a black-cloaked man during meditation was the Grim Reaper. Apparently, my death had really been a possibility.

My formal development continued in Cassadaga. During classes I experienced sensations that I remembered feeling when I was a child. I realized that I had been aware of spirit then, but had not known what it was. Eventually I was certified as a medium and ordained as a minister.

EIGHT

PHENOMENA

T hose of us who are familiar with the spirit world have experienced phenomena in some form or another. The examples that follow are fascinating accounts of spirit communication and extraordinary phenomena. Everyone who shared an experience, or three, is a trusted professional medium, with the exception of the last person mentioned. As outrageous as some of the stories may seem to a few readers, I have no reason to doubt anything they told me.

Ruth Callin, who I mentioned previously as being the first medium I ever consulted, and the Rev. Lillian Weigl were great friends. One of their many encounters together happened in the Cassadaga Hotel, where Lillian was the manager at the time. Ruth was visiting Lillian at the hotel for the weekend, having driven from Orlando. When Ruth came down to the dining area on the first morning, she found Lillian and some other people in the kitchen having tea. The first words out of her mouth were, "Good morning everyone, and who is Alice?"

Nellie, one of the maids, asked, "What room?"

"Nineteen," responded Ruth.

"Oh, yes, that was Alice Myers."

Apparently while Ruth was unpacking the night before, Alice appeared in spirit. She stated boldly to Ruth, "My name is Alice and I belong here." Ruth didn't know whether to pack her suitcase and leave or just what she should do.

Alice and her brother, Arthur, are spirits that resided in the Cassadaga Hotel at one time. Alice has since moved on to other realms, but Arthur is still there today. One night Lillian tells the story of her being in the dining room while the dishwasher, who was always the last one to leave, was sitting at the end of a large flight of stairs that led to the kitchen. The door was open to the kitchen, so Lillian could see in from the dining area. She witnessed the nightly ritual of Arthur coming down the stairs to bring the dishwasher a shot of gin. Lillian could hear the woman say, "Now you watch out, Mr. Arthur, don't you fall. Be careful now, Mr. Arthur."

Lillian asked, "Are you talking to Arthur?"

The dishwasher answered, "Yes. He brings me my gin every night."

The Rev. Arlene Sikora had a bizarre experience while traveling as a representative for the Human Development Center, an organization formed to teach and demonstrate psychic abilities to the public. She went to different colleges all over the United States, lecturing on psychic phenomena and other related subjects. While in Denver, Colorado, at St. Regis College in 1976, Arlene was one of several scheduled speakers participating in a seminar. One of the other speakers was Dr. Kendall Johnson of UCLA. Dr. Johnson was scheduled to do a morning program on Kirlian photography. Arlene had decided that she did not want to attend the morning portion, so she elected to sleep late in her dorm room.

That morning, as Arlene began to rise, strange events began to take place. The radio turned on. Arlene shut it off. The radio turned on again. She shut it off again. The overhead light came on, blinding her. She shut it off. Then the radio turned on again. Arlene unplugged it this time. The radio turned on again anyway. Now Arlene was getting spooked, so she got up and proceeded to try to take a shower.

While in the shower, all the lights went out, which really scared her. (Memories of the movie *Psycho* probably flashed in her head!) Then the lights went back on, so Arlene finished her shower. The lights went out again. Arlene thought there must be a major electrical problem in the whole college. She tried to blow-dry her hair when the lights went back on. The electricity went out again, then on and off. In the meantime, the radio and overhead light in the other room were also continually turning off and on. Arlene felt compelled to leave the room at that point.

Arlene walked to the cafeteria to eat breakfast. Suddenly, she wasn't hungry anymore, but had a strong craving for apple juice. Arlene drank about six glasses of juice. After drinking the juice, she decided to attend the Kirlian photography program. When she arrived, Dr. Johnson was telling the people in attendance how Semyon and Valentina Kirlian had developed instruments in 1939 that were used to capture the auras around living organisms, and how in 1968, Vladimar Inguskin had concluded that living organisms have a bioplasmic body identical to the aura described by mediums. Kirlian photography enables people to view the electrical fields around people's hands, he said, and to see how the aura changes when a person's mental or physical state changed. Everyone was fascinated and excited to participate in this exercise.

Arlene didn't want to participate with the others having their hands photographed by the machine, thinking perhaps her aura wasn't impressive enough. Finally, she relented. When Arlene placed only her left hand on the screen, it hurt her. No one else experienced pain, except Arlene. Having a Kirlian photograph taken is no more painful than having your picture taken by a regular camera, normally. But Arlene stated she felt like she had received an electric shock, and it was painful. Everyone accused her of being a big baby. Arlene would later learn that the machine had "backed up" intense energy into her system through her left hand, which happens to be the receiving side of the body. After some encouragement, Arlene placed both hands on the screen and was relieved this time not to experience another shock.

Five minutes later she was on the floor having contractions and what felt like seizures. Dr. Johnson walked over to her to calm her shaking body. He soon realized that she was having a kundalini experience. Arlene describes the event as feeling as if everything had backed up into her system and that electricity was dancing inside. It was explained to Arlene by Dr. Johnson that somehow, through the electric shock, she had all her "generators cleaned and cleared."

After the initial trauma had passed and Dr. Johnson spoke with her, Arlene felt like she could float. Her sensitivity became so keen that she could hear anything. She began to deliver messages to those present, and they were so accurate it was scary. Arlene said she could actually read people's minds. Arlene also channeled phenomenal healings to those in attendance. All her sensitivities apparently were amplified to a powerful intensity during this time.

Pictures were taken of Arlene's hands again. While in this electrified state, her aura was larger, brighter, and more intense. Compared to the normal aura pictures taken earlier, the photograph showed furry halos surrounding her fingers, with many lines and power points. (See the actual Kirlian photographs on the opposite page.)

In retrospect, Arlene feels that this experience was destined to happen. Since there was not an electrical problem anywhere on campus, a fact she discovered later, she cannot logically explain why the electricity was going on and off in her dorm room. The only conclusion Arlene can draw is that her guides were making sure she got to the seminar so that her body could be cleared to do the work she eventually performed. The craziness with the electricity in her room probably "charged" her in some way, causing her to drink the juice, which made her receptive to the electrical currents she was exposed to with the Kirlian photography. It took two days for Arlene to come down from this intense experience.

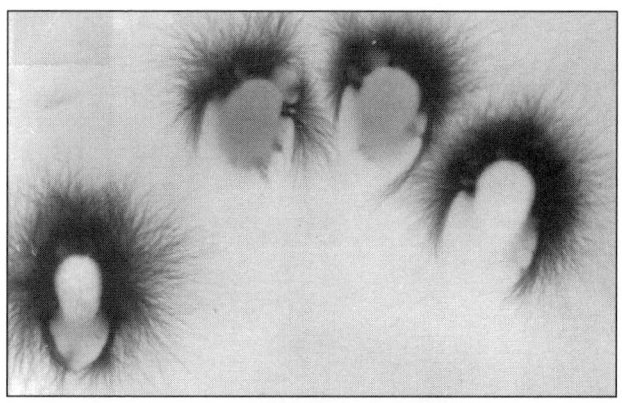

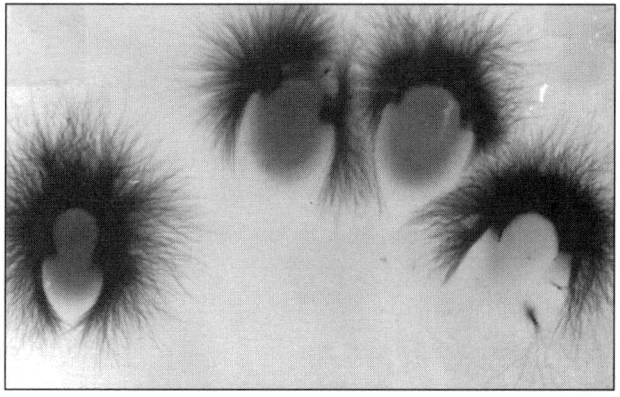

The top Kirlian photograph shows Arlene Sikora's left hand immediately prior to the initial trauma her body suffered. The bottom Kirlian photograph shows how her aura expanded after her sensitivities were intensified. The photograph where Arlene placed only her left hand on the screen, the action that apparently "sparked" the phenomena, was never found.

The Rev. Dr. Warren Hoover has been privileged to witness great phenomena by some of the best mediums in the course of his personal development. Warren studied under the magnificent Arthur Ford, among others, who is famous for the message he gave to the wife of Houdini after he had passed away. Arthur Ford was credited with being the most amazing psychic personality of that era. Ford read for such notables as Queen Maud of Norway, King George of Greece, writer Upton Sinclair, astronaut Edgar Mitchell, and writer Aldous Huxley, to name a few.

During the five years that Warren studied with Ethel Post Parrish, who was a well-known Spiritualist medium, he was fortunate to participate in several of her materialization séances. Ethel used a wooden cabinet, which was placed along the wall in the center of the séance room, and anyone who felt so inclined was entitled to inspect the cabinet prior to the séance for anything that might be considered fraudulent. A red light was the only lighting used within the room, which is a common practice at séances. Silverbell was the name of Ethel's spirit teacher, or spirit control, as it is often referred to when doing materialization work. (Ethel was later to name a Spiritualist camp in Ephrata, Pennsylvania, Silverbell, in honor of her guide. The camp is no longer in existence.)

Ethel's cabinet attendant was Lena Jefts, whose job it was to give instructions to the participants of what they could or could not do during the séance. One of

the most important rules was that no one could touch
a materialization or step in-between Ethel and the spirit
while she was in trance. The reason for this was that
ectoplasm was emanating from Ethel in order to give
form to the spirit, and the silver cord that bonded the
spirit to the medium was the life force that held the
whole process together. In full-form materializations,
the ectoplasmic silver cord sustained the temporary
ectoplasmic "earth body" of the spirit and trailed behind
the spirit form. If the connection were broken, not only
would the spirit have dematerialized instantly, but physical injury, possibly even death, could have been in-
curred by the medium.

When the spirits came out from the cabinet, they
did not have veils over their faces as some spirits did in
other séances, according to Warren, and they were surrounded by ectoplasm. Sometimes the spirits would
have stars across their forehead to show their progress
in the spirit world. When the spirits finished their visit,
every one of the materializations would walk backward
into the cabinet because of the silver cord connection.

Warren said there was no way Ethel could have left
the cabinet to imitate any of the manifestations or her
spirit teacher, Silverbell. Ethel was elderly and Silverbell, in particular, appeared to be in her twenties when
she passed on, having braids and youthful beauty. Silverbell would bounce around the room when she
talked to everyone, an impossible feat for Ethel. Sometimes there would be two, three, or four different spirit

forms walking around the floor at the same time, giving messages to individual people, further adding to Warren's belief in Ethel's genuine abilities.

Warren says that this type of phenomena simply does not exist anymore, having gone into a serious decline since 1970. Warren feels the reason is that no one wants to devote themselves to the necessary years required to develop this talent. Warren explains that after years of meditation, a person would begin with trance, followed by trumpet séances, prior to materialization.

Another lost art that some of the "old time" mediums could perform was etherealizations. This phenomena is when a vaporous spirit isn't completely formed and one can see through it. In these instances there would be enough light in the room to allow for the viewing of the vaporous substance by the participants. Warren claims there is no way any of the etherealizations he witnessed could possibly have been faked because the spirits walked around in front of people with nothing additional in the room to allow for this. We have to remember also that technology of the type that could produce a fraudulent effect such as this today, like what we might find at an amusement park, was not a reality either.

Warren also spoke with respect about Bertha Eckroad, regarding her ability to do "trumpet in the light." Trumpet in the light is a demonstration where a cone-shaped, aluminum, collapsible trumpet is used to magnify different spirit voices while the lights are on in the room. This was done by Bertha on the platform (stage).

It is far more difficult to accomplish trumpet in the light on a platform than it is in the dark of a séance room. Bertha held the small end of the trumpet in her hand while a participant would take the larger end, placing it near the ear, and the spirit would speak through the trumpet.

Johnny Reese was another old-time medium who worked at the now defunct Camp Silverbell. His spirit teacher was Bluebell, and she was known to speak out at any given time. Warren once had the experience of sitting out in the yard at Camp Silverbell talking to Johnny Reese when, suddenly, Bluebell began talking to him. The sound was coming from Johnny's solar plexus, and it was a woman's voice. Anyone who was in the vicinity heard the spirit speaking.

Sylvia DeLong attended a materialization séance with her parents many years ago. At the séance a woman in spirit came out of the cabinet to speak with her father, Leland. She said, "I am your Grandmother Mary." Leland proceeded to talk with the spirit quite naturally.

Afterward, Sylvia's mother, Hilda, voiced her doubts about what had transpired. She was a skeptic at that time with a very earthy job as a clerk of the court. All this affronted her sensibilities. Hilda asked Leland,

"What was that thing? That's ridiculous. That's a fraud. What was that on her head?"

The spirit had appeared with a towel wrapped around her head for identification purposes. Leland said to his wife, "My grandmother had such terrible headaches when she was living that she would tie a wet towel around her head." The spirit chose to show herself with the towel around her head, knowing Leland would recognize her. When they returned for the next session, Hilda felt so terrible about her mistrust that she apologized to the spirit. Grandmother Mary responded, "That's all right, child, but I had to come and I bring you these roses from my garden." Grandmother Mary held an armful of roses and everyone present could actually smell the scent of the roses.

Occasionally the DeLong family experienced phenomena within their home. One such incident was attributed to a spirit named Cloemay, a Toltec Indian, who served as a protector for the DeLongs. At the time of the incident, the family was going out seven nights a week to give lectures and teach all over Florida, often not returning until midnight. In the living room was an old-fashioned gooseneck floor lamp that was inoperable because it had become corroded and rusty. One night they came home to find the lamp on. Previously it had been humanly impossible to turn that light on. Cloemay advised them, saying, "You had to have a light, there was danger." To this day he tells Sylvia to leave the light on. "Leave the light on at night. You have nothing to fear because nothing will ever hurt you here," he told her.

When Marie and Al Lilla purchased a home in Orlando some years ago, prior to moving to Cassadaga, an antique rocking chair was one of the items left behind by the previous owners. Apparently the rocker had been handmade by the former owner's father while he lived in the garage apartment of the home. Both were quite attracted to the rocking chair, so Al refinished the wood and Marie's mother reupholstered the chair. It held a place of honor in the living room from then on.

Marie said that the rocker would, on occasion, rock for absolutely no reason. There was no breeze from an open window or air conditioning blowing in the house to cause the movement. Marie didn't pay too much attention to it, realizing it was the father who made the chair causing it to rock. This activity continued for quite a while, until one Saturday night when Marie was washing her dishes, the father made an appearance. As Marie stood in front of the sink, her Maltese dog lay with her head on Marie's foot. Out of the corner of Marie's eye she saw a man in a red shirt walk from the kitchen into the living room. Marie's first thought was that Al had changed his shirt. In the meantime, the dog went into conniptions, flying into the living room where Al laid on the couch sleeping, dressed in a white shirt. Marie followed the dog into the room, saying to Al, "Spirit past by me with a red shirt." They looked over at the rocking chair, and, sure enough, it was rocking back and forth.

They mutually decided that this wasn't going to continue. Al said in a very authoritative voice, "We understand that you made this rocker, and it is beautiful. However, you are becoming earthbound. You need to go to the light. If you are becoming attached because of this chair, we will destroy it. But if you go to the light, as long as we are alive, we will always take good care of your chair."

Two things happened after that experience. One, the rocking chair never moved independently again, and secondly, the dog refused to go into the living room. She was not particularly fond of the kitchen either after that incident. The dog would drag her dishes over to the very edge of the kitchen floor so she could stand in the dining room while she ate her food. The spirit presence scared the dog so much that this behavior continued for a long time.

The Rev. Jerry Frederich has worked with skotographs for a number of years. As a matter of fact, Jerry and I used to demonstrate this phenomena together in the late

1980s. More recently, Arlene Sikora and Jerry have teamed up for this particular presentation. This is a wonderful method in which an experienced presenter may demonstrate the continuity of life to a gathering of people.

Sheets of black and white photographic paper are cut into numerous squares, and plastic trays are prepared with the appropriate photographic development chemicals, such as developing solution, a chemical named Stop Bath, fixer, and water. Participants sit in semidarkness in a meditative state and, when they feel so inspired, place the paper square in front of a chakra, usually the solar plexus, heart, or third eye, without touching the paper to skin or clothing. Some people prefer another method, which is to simply sit with the photographic square, face up, on the palms of the hands.

After this, the paper is placed in the trays of chemicals by the facilitator and left to dry. Images of deceased relatives and friends will appear on the photographic paper.

Jerry advises that a person's intention and a relaxing meditative attitude are very important in achieving good results. Impatience brings nothing. He also feels that skotographs are not something a novice could perform properly without the guidance of an experienced teacher.

Arlene demonstrated skotographs at a workshop with Jerry shortly after her precious dog, Fenwick, had passed away. When she looked at her skotograph, it bore the unmistakable image of Fenwick, the Yorkshire terrier. Another interesting note, Fenwick loved to have his picture taken when he was on the earth plane. Whenever Arlene would take pictures during special events or on holidays, unfailingly, Fenwick would place himself in the photo. It is easy to understand why Arlene will treasure that skotograph forever.

Katherine Relda is a librarian, not a medium. She is an ordinary woman, the kind of person you might expect to pass in the grocery aisle. She does practice meditation, an activity many other normal people in the world participate in. Katherine, however, also has experienced phenomena, which is not something the average person encounters. Her experience went like this.

In 1991 Katherine acquired an abandoned Lhaso apso from a kennel. Apparently the last couple who had owned the dog fell upon circumstances that prevented them from retrieving him from the kennel. Katherine loved the dog at first sight. Mai Tai was five or six years old at the time and had had five owners because he had been raised for show, sold as a stud dog, and eventually was sold as a pet. Katherine promised Mai Tai that she would be his last owner and never abandon him.

When Mai Tai was around eleven years old, he developed kidney problems, causing his health to fail rapidly.

Although Mai Tai was on medication, he was declining, so Katherine took him to the veterinarian for overnight observation and blood tests. Katherine's husband at the time, who I will call Bob, agreed to go down to the veterinarian's office in the morning to check on Mai Tai, promising to call Katherine around 9:00 A.M. at her place of employment with an update.

The next morning Katherine was completing bills for the law firm she worked for, when, suddenly, she wasn't there. At the moment she left her body, Katherine thought perhaps she had pitched forward with her head on her desk, asleep due to exhaustion from being awake all night with worry over her dog. But then Katherine became conscious of a walking movement, and when she looked down, she saw that Mai Tai was with her and he was now a puppy. They appeared to be walking in an ocean scene that had extreme colors of blue in the sky with brilliant sunlight present. She was also aware of a Greek structure made of stone that reminded her of the Parthenon. All of a sudden, Katherine was able to observe herself at the same time she was walking around in this body. Katherine saw herself standing in the center of a stone circle up on a tower, and Mai Tai was still with her. Then a blinding light came from above, surrounding the two of them, which lifted them upward.

Katherine now found herself standing in front of the veil between the earth world and the spiritual world. She described it as appearing like a bubble, a living thing, a membrane, with shimmering colors emanating from the other side. The sounds of barking dogs came to Katherine's ears from beyond the veil. A hole opened up in the membrane big enough for Mai Tai only. He quickly ran through the hole, barking. She reached out for Mai Tai, shouting, "No!" But he was gone and she could not pass through the membrane-like veil.

In an instant, Katherine was back at her desk looking at figures again. She became conscious of the fact that she had not been asleep and still had the red pen in her hand she had been holding previously and was even writing. As soon as Katherine realized where she was, the phone rang. It was her husband and it was now 10:00 A.M., an hour later than he was supposed to have called. Bob told her he was coming to get her from work. This scared Katherine, so she asked, "How bad is it?" Bob replied that they had put Mai Tai to sleep.

After Bob picked her up, Katherine asked for more details. Bob told her that when he had talked to the veterinarian, the doctor had said that Mai Tai was failing badly and it was best to put the dog to sleep. Bob stayed with Mai Tai during the process and relayed to Katherine an unusual happening. He said the moment they gave Mai Tai the shot, there was a blinding light that surrounded Mai Tai and he knew at that moment the dog was gone. Even the veterinarian and his assistant saw the brilliant light and expressed that they had never seen anything like that before in their lives.

After Katherine shared her extraordinary experience, Bob was both amazed and relieved. He had been concerned because Katherine was unable to be there with Mai Tai, and her story showed that she had been present. Bob and Katherine both agreed that a part of Katherine had accompanied the dog when he passed into spirit, thus keeping true to her promise to Mai Tai.

This is a photograph of a fire walk that was held in Orlando, Florida. Don Zanghi, a medium from Cassadaga, took this picture just prior to him walking on the bed of coals shown. The white, round spots in the picture were visible after the photo was developed and are called orbs. They are believed to be spirit energy or possibly angels. The appearance of orbs in pictures reportedly has been occurring with expensive and inexpensive cameras alike and appears to be a phenomena that has occurred all over the U.S. in recent years. Orbs have been seen in videotapes as well.

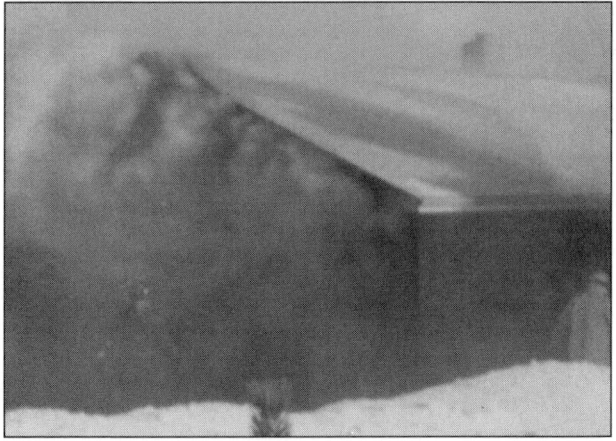

These are photographs of a house fire that erupted at Edna and Henry Brobst's home in Michigan. The top picture shows the smoke billowing out of the house. In the bottom picture, a "face" or spirit image appears in the billowing smoke, on the left side of the picture. The photos are courtesy of Edna Brobst.

NINE

NOT PLAYING
GAMES

There are different means at our disposal to experiment with when we want to communicate with spirit. One could refer to them as exercises. The following are examples of some things you might like to attempt or even practice on a regular basis. They are fun, entertaining, and can be quite enlightening. But they are not games. Please treat all communication with spirit with the greatest of respect. After all, they do not have to cooperate. If you do not participate in a manner that shows respect, spirit may simply pass you by.

Ouija Board

There are various opinions regarding the Ouija board. Some people believe that evil spirits or only low entity beings come through to communicate. I asked different mediums how they felt about the Ouija board and received very positive responses. All of them stated that it was not a game and should not be taken lightly.

Arlene disagrees with any concept of lower beings communicating through the Ouija board, claiming to have had rewarding experiences. She says that the quality of information and communication depends on the individuals using it and their intent, purpose, and spirituality. On one occasion in Arlene's experience, the information was very strong and revealing, and extremely accurate predictions were made for some people who were in the house at that time. The force, she believes, was of a high level, but because the information was too personal, in Arlene's view, she decided not to use the Ouija board again.

The Rev. Dr. Warren Hoover also believes in the validity of the Ouija board and discounts the notion that evil spirits control the board. Certainly, he feels, a mischievous spirit, or a jokester, as he calls them, can come through, but that doesn't make them evil.

When we use the Ouija board, light is sent out into the universe, the same as when we meditate, so an ignorant spirit could be attracted to us. But they aren't evil either, like some people would have you believe. Remember, mischievous and ignorant are not synonymous with evil.

Marie Lilla and her husband, Al, are firm believers in the benefits of communicating with spirit through the Ouija board. They have compiled a large notebook of communications that they have received by using the Ouija. When Al's father passed away on Christmas Eve one year, even before New Year's Eve had arrived, they were talking to his dad on the Ouija board. Marie and Al love to use the Ouija board.

Sylvia DeLong speaks about how she and her parents would use the Ouija board to receive high guidance. Sylvia has experienced many significant things: Her moving to Cassadaga was predicted through the Ouija board. But Sylvia does not recommend this practice for everyone, because some people may not appreciate the gift involved here. Beautiful things can come through, but there is potential for abuse, such as someone using it for every decision or matter in life.

We must also recognize that numerous books have been written due to the information that a spirit communicated to a human being through a Ouija board. Stewart Edward White's book, *The Betty Book*, is a good example of such communication. The most famous would be the four volumes that sprang from the Ouija board communications from Patience Worth, a discarnate spinster of Puritan extraction, to Pearl Curran and Emily Hutchings, beginning in 1913 and continuing for many years. They are *The Sorry Tale: A Story of the Time of Christ*, *Hope Trueblood*, *The Pot Upon the Wheel*, and *Light from Beyond*. The first three works were novels and the fourth, poetry. *The Sorry Tale* was 650 pages in length and was dictated through the Ouija board at a speed of 110 words a minute. That is impressive!

The Ouija board is one of many ways for a beginner to facilitate communication with spirit since it appears to be fairly easy for spirit to manipulate the pointer. However, the fact that it is not a game must be stressed. You will need to judge the quality of the messages to determine if you want to continue communicating with an entity. If it is, in fact, a spirit communication you have established, I would caution you not to be dependent upon the Ouija board, as Sylvia suggested. It is not there for every single issue in your life.

My suggestion for working the Ouija board would be to first find a willing partner. While one person may be able to work the Ouija board alone, two is far easier. It also would be ill-advised to include anyone in this practice who is not stable emotionally. Frequently, one or the other will be the stronger medium, with the additional person supplying energy.

I don't feel it really matters to the spirit world what setting is used, but atmosphere may be important to you. Therefore, I would suggest burning a purple candle and some frankincense incense to set the stage, so to speak. Soft music sufficient for meditation would also be conducive to attracting and receiving spirit.

Start by mentally flooding white light energy around the Ouija board and then the entire room. Some people like to say a prayer to invite the higher spirits. This is an excellent idea. I would suggest something like the following:

> *Universal Presence, we ask that the highest*
> *and best spirit entities be attracted to our*
> *gathering. We seek those who may enlighten*
> *us in (our daily lives; spiritual growth; the*
> *world of spirit; whatever you desire). May*
> *we be blessed with spirits who are pure in*
> *heart and deed and of the highest spiritual*
> *level. We ask this in the name of truth. And*
> *so it is (Amen, Blessed be).*

All participants should gently place their fingertips on the pointer and keep at least one hand touching at all times during the session. Questions may be posed either silently or aloud. I feel, personally, if they are spoken aloud, it stimulates the vibration of sound, which in turn will work with the energy flow. Or you can simply wait to see what is delivered to you. Begin the procedure by speaking aloud to the spirit world to encourage movement of the pointer, saying something like, "Are you there, spirit?" or "Welcome, spirit, please begin." As in any effort to establish a relationship with spirit, ask questions of the spirit force: "What is your name? Where are you from? When were you born?"

Frequently spirit will work so rapidly that it is helpful to have a third person present to write down the letters as they are given. This avoids confusion over the meaning of the message. All the communications should be kept in a notebook or journal. Over the months it will be interesting to review the information you received. If at any time communication seems to be going nowhere, you can ask to have another spirit come through. If an unenlightened spirit comes in, send it to the white light with a prayer of blessing. Maintain a positive attitude and a sober mind. Remember, like attracts like. And always express aloud your gratitude to each entity who comes forth.

Inspirational and Automatic Writing

These are two tools you might wish to pursue in your spiritual development. Inspirational writing is where you receive thoughts while in a meditative state. What-ever comes into your head, write it down, whether it makes sense or not. It is common when sitting in devel-opment classes to be told, "Say your first thought. Don't think about it." This encourages the energy flow without the interference of your own thoughts to block the stream of information that can flow from spirit. You are getting out of your own way, so to speak. When you read what has come through afterward, you may find some pearls of wisdom within the lines you have jotted down.

Automatic writing is when a spirit has taken some sort of control over what is written. This is usually done in a meditative or trance state while the hand is inde-pendently writing what spirit wants to convey. There would not be conscious knowledge of what is being delivered from the spirit world while this is happening.

In even rarer circumstances, there are instances where an individual has sat with a pencil and paper while they are talking on the telephone and spirit uses the free hand to write. The person is totally unaware of what is being written, only cognizant of his or her conversation with the individual on the other end of the telephone line. This is possible because the mind is so totally focused that the person is open to being a free-flowing channel. As I said before, getting out of your own way.

Some people are capable of writing automatically with the opposite hand that they normally use for writing. Others will find their penmanship changing dramatically or that they even write words in another language that is foreign to them. Warren Hoover thinks automatic writing is a good method to use when trying to establish communication, and Diane Davis agrees. However, inspirational writing will come easier. Here is what I would suggest.

Select a time when you can remain undisturbed by animals or people. Gather together the materials you will need, which are a tablet and a pen or pencil. Light a blue or white candle, burn some of your favorite incense, and play appropriate music for meditation.

Close your eyes and breathe deeply through the nose and exhale through the lips. Repeat this two more times. Concentrate on different areas of your body, starting with the feet. Silently tell each area to relax as you slowly work your way upward. Then sit quietly listening to the music for a few minutes. See what begins to happen. If thoughts pop into your head, write them down. As you practice, it will become easier. Eventually, you may be able to go deep enough into meditation that spirit will begin to work through your hand. Also, you may wish to attempt to receive communication at the same time you are talking on the phone, as was mentioned earlier.

Automatic Drawing

Automatic drawing is another tool. Let me share Arlene Sikora's experience with you. At the time, Arlene was a senior counselor at a high school. The seniors had already graduated for the school year, which meant that Arlene had completed her records. However, the rest of the school was still in session, so Arlene was required to be in attendance. This presented Arlene with a lot of free time, so she filled the hours by drawing with charcoal on newsprint. This activity was totally out of character for Arlene since she had no previous artistic ability whatsoever.

Arlene felt she was being inspired. She started by drawing eyes, never knowing what the picture would become later: a woman, man, or child. She collected twenty-seven caricatures, as she calls them. One in particular was an obvious rendering of a policeman, another a female belly dancer. The faces were exceptionally detailed.

After completing these drawings, Arlene did another workshop for the Human Development Center, this time in Massachusetts. An amazing thing happened on the first day of the class. Twenty-seven people attended her workshop, and they were the exact same faces she had drawn previously, right down to a cop and a woman who was taking belly-dancing classes. Arlene had no previous information about the people who would be attending her class when she did the drawings, and certainly could not have known that one woman was taking belly-dancing lessons. Arlene gave the pictures to each person, explaining that she had received them during meditation.

Arlene knew she was not the one actually drawing the pictures. Most of the drawings, but not all of them, were signed by a spirit named David. During this time, Arlene began to notice her personality changing. Arlene could be described as an assertive person, but not flippant and cocky in attitude. However, she began to exhibit these traits and felt that it was David's influence from spirit causing her to behave in this manner.

Arlene believed David was satisfying his ego needs through her with his art. She finally addressed David by saying if he wasn't willing to grow spiritually while working with her, they would not have an opportunity to continue working together. David was furious. After the confrontation, he refused to work with Arlene on a spiritual basis, so she chose not to participate with him and his art. David left her and she has not picked up a pencil to draw since.

If you wish to attempt automatic drawing, select a time and place where you will not be disturbed. Assemble drawing paper and either charcoal, colored pencils, or pastels, whichever you feel is best suited for you. Personally, I would recommend colored pencils or even a regular No. 2 pencil, because charcoal is messy. Or you can choose a combination of the colored pencils and pastels—just use what is comfortable for you. Also, light a blue candle and burn rose incense while playing soft music suitable for meditation.

Close your eyes and enter a meditative state by concentrating on your breathing. Begin by breathing deeply and then exhaling audibly. Do this three times. Then simply focus on your normal breathing. Depending how advanced you are in meditation, you may wish to take yourself on a mental journey to your favorite place in nature. Allow sufficient time to walk among the various forms of nature present there. If this is difficult to do, I would suggest playing a guided imagery tape to bring you into a meditative state.

Next, try one of these two methods. With closed eyes, have your hand poised on top of the paper with your drawing instrument in hand and wait to see what happens. Or, open your eyes and see how you are guided to proceed.

I would not anticipate any of these writing/drawing methods producing extraordinary results with the first attempt. Patience will be needed to develop this talent, as with all psychic abilities.

Table Tipping

Sylvia DeLong and her parents employed table tipping as a device to contact spirits. Table tipping is where one or more people sit around a wooden table for the purpose of having it move, rap, or raise up and down on one or more legs as a sign from spirit to answer yes or no to questions asked by the participants. Sylvia said that a different band of spirits would work with them during these sessions, mostly Native Americans, than normally communicated with the family.

Sylvia feels this is an excellent way to contact spirit besides being a means to receive confirmation of clairvoyance. When the family participated in table tipping, as the spirit was operating the table, Sylvia would describe what the spirit looked like as she saw it in her mind. The table would respond with a yes or no answer as to her accuracy. Sylvia's father did not use any lights when doing this method. Some people use a blue or red light, or even a candle.

I often use table tipping in my development classes to show another form of communication with the spirit world. The table I use is a wooden card table that my parents played cards on with friends when they were young. It is over fifty years old and, because it is natural wood and an antique, I believe it is very receptive to spirits. My father especially enjoys communicating with me on the table, which is understandable since it was his table.

On several occasions, my sister, who was stillborn, has come through. The first time that happened I was quite taken aback. Being a believer in reincarnation, I thought she would have been in human form by now, since it has been over forty years since her birth. But, then again, time is only important to us on the earth plane, not the spirit world.

A demonstration of the phenomena of table tipping was filmed by a local news crew in the séance room of our church. The female newscaster participated with my class and, much to her amazement and that of the woman filming the activity, the table responded extremely well. The newscaster definitely identified her father as one of the spirits operating the table. Her father came through with such strength that the table literally slid around the entire room. We had to run to keep up with it at times, and some of the people had to bow out because it became difficult to continue the fast pace. But that did not affect the intensity of the energy flow. With the newscaster and only one other person participating, her father still manipulated the table across the room. When the table stopped moving in such a fast manner, she was able to ask questions. The information she received to her questions was consoling to her. The newscaster became a true believer in table tipping.

My first suggestion for participating in table tipping would be to gather numerous people together who are of like mind. If someone is a skeptic, they can pull the energy down to the point where nothing will happen. During one session in a particular class I was giving, the table refused to budge. The only difference between this session and the others the class had participated in was the inclusion of one man. When we asked him to lift his hands from the table and step back to the wall, the table began to respond. So, it is very important to bring together friends and acquaintances who are agreeable with each other and have an open mind regarding what may happen.

The number of people who participate will probably depend on the size of your table. My card table accommodates six people seated, however, as many as ten people can stand around the card table. A dining room table would allow for a larger group participation, but I would suggest that you start with something smaller. While a large, heavy table can bounce around the room, raise up on one leg, and even levitate, it is much easier with a small table, plus there is less damage to the floor.

Take the phone off the hook, close any connections to cell phones or beepers, and do not wear watches that audibly announce the time or beep. Although table tipping can be done in the dark, it is usually best and more comfortable when done in low lighting. Total darkness can make some people feel uneasy. Besides, most people enjoy seeing the table movements and the reactions on each other's faces that low lighting can provide. Candle light is soft and very conducive, as would be a lamp with a control to adjust the intensity, such as halogen lighting. However, it would be best to have the candle in a wall sconce in case the spirits decide to maneuver the table around the room. If table tipping is being conducted in a room where other furniture is present, place the candle on another piece of furniture that is heavy to avoid the risk of it being jostled and falling over, causing a fire. The same would hold true for the halogen lighting. The lamp would need to be placed in an area where it cannot be pushed over. Overhead lighting is always a good method to provide subtle lighting too, if you have that sort of light fixture.

All parties should lightly place their fingertips on the top of the table. In séances held in the early days of Spiritualism, participants would spread out their fingers across the table top, place their own thumbs together, and rest their pinkie fingers so they touched the person on either side. It was felt that they were connecting their personal energy by using this method. It really is not necessary to do this, but if this method appeals to you, follow that direction. It is important that no one remove both of their hands from the table. If you need to scratch or cough, lift one hand only and replace it when you are finished.

When everyone is ready, a prayer should be said aloud by one person, similar to the following:

> *Infinite Intelligence, we lovingly invite our*
> *relatives and friends who are on the spirit*

*side of life to communicate with us now. We
welcome their attendance and ask that they
communicate messages to us. We give grateful thanks for their presence today (tonight).
We ask this in the name of truth, Amen (And
so it is, so be it).*

Have everyone close their eyes and visualize white
light energy flooding the room.

The next step is to raise the vibration, and this is
done best by sound. In other words, sing! It doesn't
have to be pretty, just loud. The *Battle Hymn of the
Republic* is a good one, or even *Row, Row, Row Your
Boat*. Sometimes my class had more success with religious songs. It probably depends upon the spirits you
are attempting to attract. *Amazing Grace* is a good
hymn to try. I have had really good success with, of all
songs, *Do Wah Ditty, Ditty, Dum Ditty Do*! Don't worry
if you start laughing either. Spirit likes laughter. It cre-
ates a happy vibration.

It may take up to thirty minutes the first time you
attempt table tipping before you receive any vibration
from the table. You also need to be prepared for a total
no-show. However, faster results may happen. It will
depend on who is participating. There simply are no
guarantees, especially the first time.

What you should anticipate is feeling a slight vibration from the table, perhaps a rap or knock. A cracking
sound could come from the table, walls, or ceiling, then
movement should follow. The table could shimmy or

move from side to side. It may lift one leg off the floor, which would then thump down. As the energy builds, the table should get more raucous. It can start sliding across the room, moving erratically, and thumping up and down on one or two legs. Sometimes a table will levitate, although I haven't been privileged to experience that myself. If you are chasing after the table, this is not the time to ask questions.

When it appears that communication can begin, ask the spirit to show you a sign for yes. The table will either move back and forth, sideways, or one or two legs will rise off the floor. Once you have established what yes is, ask for the sign of no. The table may move in the opposite direction, or it may thump the floor twice for no as opposed to once for yes. I've even experienced a lack of movement for a no answer, while a yes answer would be demonstrated by a table leg rising up and down.

After yes and no have been established, begin to ascertain who is working the table. I used to ask the spirit, "Do you have a message for Marie?" If the table is quiet, I would ask if the spirit had a message for another of the students. We proceeded like this until the spirit responded to someone's name. Often we would sense who the message was for.

Whoever was to be the recipient of a message would ask the spirit if it was his or her uncle, for instance. By process of elimination, it was possible to determine which friend or relative was there. Then he or she would ask a question of the spirit, and possibly several more until the communication faded. When the table ceased to move, we would ask the spirit, "Are you still with us, Uncle Ben?" The table would not move, so we knew the spirit had gone on. At this point we would ask aloud for another spirit to come forth. When the table started rocking again, we would repeat the whole process. Eventually we recognized the energy of some of the spirits who frequented our gatherings regularly.

Other areas of sensitivity can be explored while doing table tipping, as Sylvia suggested. Practice determining who the spirit wants to contact, what relative is present in spirit, and the accuracy of your perception of the physical appearance of the spirit.

When the table ceases to be active, it is time to close the session. Give a brief prayer of thanks for the spirit visits received. Then lift your hands from the table to break the connection.

During the series of classes I was teaching when these examples occurred, I found it interesting how one session would differ from another. Sometimes one person would attract a lot of spirits and someone else would receive none. Other times everyone received at least one visitation and sometimes more. No matter how large or small our successes were, we always expressed our gratitude to the spirits for coming. We thanked each one when they arrived and gave thanks again out loud when they left. Gratitude is very important. We must remember that they don't have to communicate with us.

The most important thing to remember is not to get discouraged if the table doesn't bounce around the room the first time you attempt table tipping or no spirits communicate. Sometimes the spirits are not in the mood to visit, the energy needs to build among the group a few times in order to receive the messages, or one person could be sabotaging the group's efforts. It may simply take some practice. As to a table bouncing around the room, yours may never do that. You have to consider that my class was conducted in a séance room that was well "seasoned" since the 1920s by spiritual activities.

TEN

GETTING
STARTED

In order to receive communication from spirit, you have to be earnest and dedicated. Communication may not happen after just one or two attempts. Therefore, it is possible to become frustrated with the process, unless you are aware of some particulars. This chapter will show you how to prepare for communication and what to anticipate as a normal happening.

The Rev. Jerry Frederich feels intention and motivation are key to communication. Sometimes we are seeking to heal ourselves emotionally or physically, uplift our spirits, or clear up confusion in our lives. We may wish to be in touch with relatives who have passed because we require confirmation about their well-being. Curiosity can lead one to meditate for communication with spirit.

Understanding the personal motivation definitely aids the process of communication. Ask yourself, "Why? What is my purpose for learning to communicate with spirit?" A positive purpose will receive the best results.

Jerry feels that meditation is God's Internet. It is where one is using the subconscious as the vehicle to connect with the Source, Universal Mind, God. We could use the analogy of moving the mouse so the little cursor on the computer screen makes a connection to the Internet. Information is sought, information is received. We benefit from the communication and act accordingly.

Consistency is important if you want to establish communication with your spirit teachers. Consider for a moment how you would feel if someone declared that he or she wanted to be your friend. He or she desired to talk to you, be a companion, and seek your counsel on occasion, like friends often do. But this friend could not be depended on to keep appointments. Every time you scheduled a luncheon together or shopping spree, your friend couldn't be bothered to show up. I don't imagine that you would tolerate this behavior in a so-called friend. It works the same with the spirit world.

If you truly want to communicate through meditation, you need to keep a schedule. I have often heard it referred to as keeping a date with spirit. Select a time during the morning, day, or evening to meditate, and then be prepared to meditate at that time each day.

Don't put it off until later or decide to wait until the next day. Honor your commitment, otherwise spirit may not bother to come.

Sylvia DeLong sits twice a day in meditation for perhaps ten minutes. Sometimes she receives nothing and other days she receives abundant communications. Ten minutes is an adequate amount of time in which to meditate. It is not an unreasonable or inconvenient length of time to devote to your spiritual growth. If you have more time available on certain days, twenty or thirty minutes is also a good time frame. The length of time will depend a lot on your personal schedule, as will the time of day. Spirit is flexible about those matters.

Many mediums feel that meditation upon arising is a wonderful way to begin a new day. Before the newspaper is read or the television is turned on, they seek the silence prior to worldly contaminations. Being so newly returned to the world from the sleep state is a very conducive time for receiving spirit communication. However, for those who must hustle in the morning hours to make it to work on time, this may not be the best period for you. People have been known to fall back asleep while meditating in the morning, consequently causing them to be late for work or appointments. Not a good way to start the day!

The afternoon is usually too busy for most folks to meditate, although there are exceptions. During the lunch hour, some people are able to steal away a period of private time in which to seek the silence. I know of several women who sit in a park during their lunchtime and meditate. Of course, this is Florida I'm talking about. During certain times of the year, that would be an impossibility in northern states. One mother, who is a client of mine, finds her private time while her baby naps in the afternoon. You will have to be the judge if the afternoon hours are appropriate for you.

Meditating right after dinner can make anyone uncomfortable and produce distracting noises. I remember in one class I taught, all six of the girls who normally attended decided to eat a spaghetti dinner prior to coming to my class. All through the session, their stomachs groaned and gurgled, and they held back belches. They learned that it is not a good idea to eat a heavy meal prior to meditation.

Most people meditate in the evening hours. I found that the recommended time, according to old-time Spiritualist books, was 8:00 P.M. Apparently this time was considered to be long enough after the dinner hour and not too close to bedtime, which is good advice. Most of the development classes I attended during my unfoldment were held at 7:30 P.M. By the time the lesson was delivered, it was 8:00 P.M. when we actually began our meditation. Perfect timing.

If we meditate just prior to going to sleep, we run the same risk as in the morning—the potential to fall asleep. However, this is still a good time to meditate, but we must remember to sit in a chair rather than lie on the bed. As a matter of fact, I don't recommend lying in bed at anytime to meditate. We simply get too comfortable, and, what is a bed for? To sleep in, of course. Psychologically, we are trained to sleep, not meditate, in bed. We set ourselves up for a missed session if we meditate in bed.

A bedtime meditation is a good method for unwinding from the day's events. We can record our experiences from the meditation in a journal and write about what we learned from life in general that day. Also, we can record how the previous night's meditation assisted us during our day when that is appropriate. We may find that we sleep better, too, after a relaxing meditation.

I would suggest that you experiment with different times in order to find the one that is most suitable for you. It is also important to choose a time when you will not be disturbed. A meowing cat in the room or a barking dog outside is not conducive to meditation. Neither is an impatient partner knocking on the closed door, inquiring when you are coming to bed.

Some ground rules may need to be established so that you can maintain a peaceful area. If children, spouses, or roommates are an issue to deal with, a sign posted on the door stating "Meditating: Do not disturb unless the house is burning down" is usually sufficient to get your point across. Inform everyone that once that sign goes up, you are not taking phone calls, answering the door, talking to anyone, or doing anything that requires your attention. Trust me, humans are just as trainable as pets.

Once you have discovered the best time for your meditation, set your date with spirit and keep it. And don't you dare allow yourself to feel guilty for allotting time for yourself. After all, everyone deserves some personal moments. Life will wait until you exit from the room. Consider this: If you do not treat yourself properly, how can you expect to develop into the best "you" you are capable of becoming? The better you are, the more wisdom and strength you have to draw upon for the support of your friends, family, and partners.

Warren Hoover finds it so rewarding to communicate with his spirit teachers. His experience has been that they reveal all kinds of things about themselves, such as their name, where they were born, their profession, the time in history they lived, anything at all. It is similar to forming a new friendship. The spirits we seek to contact have lived in human form, so treat them as you would any other friend. Ask them questions, thank them for their assistance, ask the spirit to speaker slower, louder, more clearly, or not to stand so close. Warren says that the more you work with your spirit teachers, the more familiar they will become to you. Practice makes perfect. It's like exercising a muscle, I always say. The more you lift that weight over time, the stronger that bicep becomes. The more you meditate, the stronger the communication will become with spirit.

After Arlene Sikora started development classes and practicing meditation, she became discouraged because

nothing seemed to be happening. No lights, no awareness of spirit, nothing. One night as she lay in bed and
began to pray, she spoke to spirit in her head, saying,
"And they told me you would make yourself known to
me . . . ," and before she could complete the thought,
the softest, most beautiful female voice said, "You've
never asked."

The spirit told Arlene that she had been around for
a long time, but Arlene had not asked for her to come
forward. It was as simple as that. The beautiful spirit
then took Arlene on an out-of-body "journey of introduction" into the world of spirit. Arlene viewed build-
ings and things in the spirit world that she had no
prior conception of. It was a truly rewarding experience and an enlightening event. The spirit was a Native
American and she is with Arlene to this day.

When you begin to meditate for the purpose of contacting spirit, you may or may not experience abnor-
mal happenings. Arlene had several experiences that
were quite outstanding. I would not consider her three
events standard occurrences, nor should you anticipate
anything like them manifesting in your home. Most
people will receive a few unexplained knocks or perhaps a small object will be found in another location.
That's normal. What spirit demonstrated in Arlene's
home was extraordinary.

Arlene routinely placed a candle in a holder in the
center of an old oak claw-foot table when she meditated. She would sit in front of the table, asking for

truth and the highest and the best to come through. One night the candle moved across the table, then back, to the side, back to center, and then to the other side of the table. When it was done moving around, Arlene realized that it had formed the sign of a cross. She never received an explanation for this.

An interesting series of events started one night when Arlene awoke to the sound of voices in the living room. Being fully awake with her eyes open, Arlene listened to the sounds of a party going on in the next room—a spirit party. Arlene explained the incident by saying it was like thirty people were all talking at once. She could not understand what they were saying individually, but they were having one heck of a good time. She marched out to the living room to tell them to quiet down and ask why she wasn't included. No explanation. This was only the beginning. Arlene estimates this "party" occurred twenty times.

In the living room Arlene had four little footstools individually marked with an ace, a club, a diamond, and a heart that were positioned in specific areas by the fireplace. Every night when a party occurred, she would go out into the living room and usually find the footstools scattered around the room. She had a collection of Pilgrim glass in the den area that also received some unwanted attention from the spirits. Whenever the stools were moved, Arlene would also find the glassware placed on the floor, unbroken.

Understandably, it became an irritating situation to Arlene—she couldn't get any sleep! She told the spirits if she couldn't be included in the party, she wanted them to find another place for their activity. So they went away. These were definitely mischievous spirits.

Early in Arlene's exploration and experimentation stage of her development, she spent some time with her godmother's family (who I mentioned previously in the book). One night the four daughters and Arlene were upstairs in the family's home. They decided it would be fun to pray the rosary to see if they could get the spirits to do something, "Show me what you can do, spirit." Soon after that request, they started hearing raps on the walls. Not little snaps, but knocks emanating from the walls and even in between the walls. It was such an obvious noise, like a percussion symphony performing throughout the house. The family had been in their home for many years, so the noise could not have been explained away as the house settling. There were so many raps that the girls' father came running upstairs to see what all the commotion was about. He appeared at the door, white-faced and scared, asking what was happening. He didn't appreciate their answer.

Once spirit begins to communicate with you in meditation, they may also choose to do so when you are at work, for instance, or shopping at the grocery store. They will find ways to intuitively impress you. For Sylvia DeLong, it is a gut feeling emanating from her solar plexus when her intuition is trying to tell her something. This is a clear sign not to be dismissed because something is amiss. For me, it is like feeling a thought suddenly strike into my head. I can't help but notice this thought because it comes from out of the blue, and it feels like it hits me, literally, inside my head.

It is important to understand that the guidance we receive from the spirit world is not meant to take away our free will. We have the freedom of choice to accept or reject the information we receive. As I said before, we are the ones in control. We may not agree with the advice that is being given to us. After all, we are all individuals with opinions, experiences, and various beliefs, and sometimes we think we know best. Like Frank Sinatra used to sing, "I did it my way." We are free to choose whatever path we want, and this is a good thing.

Just because we have the ability to make choices, though, does not necessarily mean we will make the wisest ones in every circumstance. Sometimes we goof. Communication with the spirit world does not promise us a charmed life, mistake free. It is simply guidance and direction. How many times have we sought advice from a parental figure or friend? We asked for information, we received information. And then we made the final decision. Sometimes we chose well and, of course, sometimes we didn't.

Communication with spirit is not intended to replace our decision-making processes or common sense. Only we can make our own decisions. We are on the earth plane to experience our own individual karma. Sometimes our personal development requires that we make mistakes. Sylvia acknowledges that her guides have occasionally allowed her to make errors. From these so-called mistakes, we learn the best lessons for our growth.

Personally, I do not believe that we make mistakes in our lives. My feeling is that we may make inappropriate choices that harm us or others, but never mistakes. When bad things happen due to the choices we make, we learn. When chaos enters our lives due to the choices we make, we can grow beyond the experience. When disappointment wraps us within a ball of despair, we learn not to repeat that action. That's not a bad thing. It's growth.

It is unwise to become unnecessarily dependent upon a spirit. Should this happen, the entity has the option to take a leave of absence or never return. A medium I was acquainted with became very dependent upon the principle guide she worked with when she was giving readings. Even during the time she spent going about her normal affairs, she was constantly looking to him for guidance in every matter and circumstance. She was not conducting her own life, preferring to allow the guide to make all her decisions. When this behavior continued and no attempt was made by the medium to correct the situation, the guide finally made himself unavailable to her. Even during the medium's private meditations, he didn't come.

Eventually the entity did return when he felt the medium had learned the lesson of overdependence.

Once communication has been established, a guide may give you an exercise to see if you are paying attention and following your intuition. Arlene Sikora gave me a personal and humorous example of how spirit tested her.

On a rainy, snowy, cold day in Maine, Arlene pulled up to a store entrance to allow her passenger to exit from her car so they would not get soaked by the weather. She pulled forward somewhat and waited, adjusting her seat into a semireclining position. While she was waiting, the sound of a spirit voice clearly came from nowhere. Spirit said, "There's a wad of money under the car." Arlene thought, *Yeah, yeah*, and ignored it. The same voice came again. "There's a wad of money under the car." Understandably, Arlene had no intention of getting out of the car in the nasty rain and cold to check out anything so ridiculous as the idea of money being under the car. Then she heard spirit say, "We're telling you, and we're not telling you again, there's a wad of money under the car." Reluctantly, Arlene moved the car forward, got out, and walked around to the back of the car. Sure enough, there lay a wad of money with a rubber band around it. However, it was all Monopoly game money. Spirit got her!

Arlene believes spirit was testing her to see if she would follow through with the instructions she received. While she did pay attention to spirit, Arlene knows now she should have asked for more information, such as if it was real spending money, or is it Chinese yen. Arlene got a good laugh out of it later. This incident also shows that spirit can have a sense of humor.

Louis Gates' mother was a full-blooded Seneca Indian and had the gift of prophecy from birth. She taught Louis from the time he was four years old how to connect with spirit. One important piece of advice she relayed to her son was, "Get yourself out of the way, get your thoughts completely out of the way."

By detaching ourselves from the question or circumstance at hand, we are freeing up our receiving channel so that we are able to communicate with spirit. This is a good example where the principle "your first thought" is appropriate. No analyzation, no thoughts of "oh, this can't be right" allowed. The first thought is usually the correct one. When our brains are buzzing over thoughts about the day's events or what is anticipated tomorrow, we are not getting out of our way. We are, instead, standing squarely in front of our objective, blocking any hope of success.

It is usually easier to detach from a situation when we are not personally involved in the outcome, especially when it has to do with affairs of the heart. Some years ago I knew a medium who had been involved with a woman for over a year, and he wanted to know if they would marry. In order to detach from the emotions of the situation, he focused on her future instead of his. When he saw that she would become involved with other people and circumstances than those that were current, he knew that their relationship would not lead to marriage.

The ability to concentrate is helpful when trying to be detached. We are, through the act of concentration, bringing our minds to a point, focusing the attention on the question at hand. If our thoughts are scattered in twenty directions, it is impossible to be an open receiver for spirit. Additionally, our surroundings may not always be perfect. When a medium is giving a reading, the ideal is a quiet environment. However, as in any neighborhood, airplanes do pass overhead. Garbage trucks also make loud rumbling noises, mechanical sounds, and even the crashing of glass can occur. We cannot allow ourselves to be distracted by theses noises or any others. Once you have accomplished a certain amount of training, it will be possible to recognize the presence of unwanted sounds but not be bothered by them.

One method of learning concentration is to visualize a simple object. A round red ball, a candle flame, or a religious symbol, such as a cross or the Star of David, are good examples. The idea is to hold that vision in your mind without allowing your thoughts to stray. Every time you start to think about your dog playing with the ball, for instance, you must immediately bring your focus back to the red ball. With practice, your powers of concentration will greatly improve and so will your ability to detach.

In most situations we can pose a question during meditation and receive a response from spirit. It is unlikely the answer will come from a booming voice stating, "Yes!" or "No!" For some people, the right side of the body is sensitive to a yes answer and the left side a no. When they present a question during meditation, they try to attune to one side of their body and then the other. Whichever side feels the most sensitive is their answer.

Spirit may give us a symbol to decipher or a scene to intuit the meaning of as we observe it being played out in our minds. Others receive answers by just getting an intuitive feeling: it feels like yes, it feels like no, or wait a while to see how other events play out first.

If during meditation you frequently receive symbols, one of my suggestions would be to purchase a book on symbology to help you interpret what you are receiving from spirit. You will find that most books are geared toward the interpretation of symbols received while dreaming, which equally apply to symbols received during meditation. (Please see the "Suggested Reading" section in the back of the book. My favorite for symbolism is by Betty Bethards.) A book on symbols gives a foundation to work with but is not intended to be an absolute. An interpretation found in a book does not mean it is going to be 100 percent correct for you. Some books on symbols give interpretations that are psychoanalytical or pertain to ancient symbology. I prefer the metaphysical interpretations myself. There are numerous ways we can personally respond to a symbol, so it is important to additionally consider your own feelings. If the suggestion given in a book does not feel appropriate to your particular life experiences, ask that you be shown, in meditation later, what the answer is for you.

The symbol of a baby is common to see during meditation. A baby usually has one of two meanings. The first is obvious: Someone is literally going to have a baby in the future or is pregnant now. The other interpretation is that you are in or on the verge of something new, a beginning. In other words, the birth of something, such as a new idea for a novel or an ingenious plan for a new business venture. When I see this symbol during a reading, I have learned how it "feels" when I am being told that my client is pregnant or going to be. I also have learned how it "feels" when the meaning is a new venture. It takes practice to interpret a baby symbol correctly. I have not heard any medium say that a baby symbol means anything different than what I have stated, however, there is always a first time. Perhaps a baby symbol will mean something totally different for you.

We are all unique beings with individual personalities who are walking diverse paths, so it is unlikely that we will interpret identically. Always pay attention to how you feel about a symbol. What emotions does it evoke? What does that sign indicate to you personally? Are there universally accepted messages associated with a particular symbol?

If you saw in meditation a black cat, would this be a sign to you of bad luck coming, superstitious thinking in some people's minds, or would the cat remind you of your favorite family pet? Suppose a snake was in your meditation, near a person you knew. Would this give you a repulsive feeling, be a warning of a possible slippery character, or impress upon you the cleverness of this individual? All symbols cannot have the exact same meaning for all people. If one person loves snakes and another feels revulsion, how could each interpret the same meaning from that symbol? Obviously, they can't. Feel what is correct for you.

Do not be disappointed if spirit does not immediately relay a message to your question. Sometimes the answer will come later—in three minutes, three hours, three days, or three weeks. Other times the answer will spring from the front page of a newspaper two days later. A headline catches your eye and is exactly what you are seeking. Many people automatically discount the message when it comes in this fashion. It's just too easy. They think, "Oh, it can't be that. This is a coincidence." No, it's not. That's the answer right in front of you. It is important to remain open as to how you will receive an answer to a question and be aware that there are many unique ways in which to receive. Remember George Harrison singing on the radio and the motorcyclist riding by me with "Do It" printed on his T-shirt? That was not a coincidence—it was the answer to my question.

I would recommend keeping a record of your communications in a journal. By referring back to it, you will discover how you have grown and the accuracy of your encounters. It would be impossible to remember everything you receive from spirit. A journal is also a great means to work through a question. Sometimes spirit will give us the answer we seek from the journaling method. As we are writing out our dilemma on the pages, spirit is helping us sort through the situation. Suddenly, it occurs to us why we are in this particular pickle. Spirit shows how we created it ourselves.

Marie Lilla believes that an open mind is mandatory when seeking to communicate with spirit. In meditation, we do not always see what we anticipate. I have a saying that applies to a great many situations in life: "Just because you think it, doesn't make it so."

We have all been so conditioned from childhood as to what is correct, acceptable, permissible, and real that sometimes our beliefs interfere with our openness to new concepts. To emphasize my point, when I was drawing a spirit guide for a client in the late 1980s, a being from outer space came through as her guide. At the time I had no opinion about life forms on other planets nor any interest in the subject. But there "she" was, definitely an alien being. I was quite surprised by this turn of events, but I remained open and did not dismiss the image I saw. So, be open!

Marie finds it beneficial upon arising each morning to greet her spirit relatives and teachers. She goes down the whole list in her head saying, "Good morning," and finishing with, "And everyone else!" If you want spirit to look out for you, it is a good idea to be nice to them. After all, what goes around, comes around.

ELEVEN

MEDITATIONS FOR COMMUNICATION

Now that you have read everything necessary to prepare for the experience of meeting a spirit teacher, it is time to meditate for that purpose. The following meditations are designed to facilitate communication with a guide. Read them over and tape each meditation on one side of a ninety-minute audiotape. By using ninety-minute tapes, each meditation will fit easily onto one side, and you won't run the risk of the tape player turning off before you are done and startling you back into a conscious state. Speak slowly when you are taping and always allow enough time to follow the instructions being given. I have indicated where to allow for time by placing the word "pause" in parenthesis.

It is possible that you will respond more to one meditation than another, so that is why I created three. On the other hand, it is possible that you will receive a different guide from each meditation. If this doesn't happen right away, over time you may find that to be your eventual outcome. After all, each of us has more than one guide. These meditations can be used over and over through the years whenever you feel the need to seek another guiding influence.

If this is the first time you have ever meditated, do not allow yourself to become discouraged if afterward you feel that you have had a nice, relaxing journey somewhere but, unfortunately, did not see, feel, or hear a spirit guide. It took the Rev. Jerry Frederich six months of meditation in a development class before he had any results, and even then all he saw was a field of white and heard a humming in the air. It was two years after that before he received a visual. Even so, Jerry developed into a fine reader. It is also important to remember, Jerry is not you. Jerry was a skeptical person, had a hyper personality, and a very "busy" mind. He did not easily relax into a quiet, meditative state and a receptive demeanor to achieve spirit communication.

You will develop at your own appropriate rate. If nothing much happens during the first attempt, time will change that. The following day, select another meditation, then continue using a different tape each day until you have results, even if you start again with the first meditation and go through each one a second time.

Do not allow yourself to feel that you are doing something wrong. Everyone is an individual. We respond in our own unique ways at the proper times for us. Also, even if you do have a wonderful first attempt, do not be discouraged if it wasn't what you expected. To do so would diminish your experience. For instance, suppose you anticipated seeing or hearing a spirit, but only felt the presence of an entity. Simply feeling a presence is a highly significant event! Just because it did not occur the way you had hoped is not an indication of failure. As a matter of fact, there is no such thing as a failed attempt. Remember that spirit also plays a part in this communication. You are not doing this alone. If you have never sought out a spirit's attention, what makes you think they are lined up to respond to your call the very first time? It can happen, but it is just as likely it won't. So do not be unduly harsh with yourself.

If you are fortunate to see a spirit during meditation, do not be disappointed if the spirit does not tell you his or her name or give you all the details that are possible to receive from a spirit teacher. (The terms "him or her" and "he or she" are used here because spirits will appear as one of the genders they incarnated as previously.) Perhaps the spirit does not want to reveal information about him or herself until he or she knows you better. As you continue to work with a spirit, he or she will probably open up to you. And then again, maybe he or she never will reveal certain details. That is not a fault of yours, but rather, the choice of the spirit. Enjoy what you do receive and go with the flow. All things happen as they are supposed to. All things unfold when the time is appropriate for each of us.

For all your meditations, I would suggest lighting a candle. Select light blue for overall meditation and inspiration. Indigo blue and purple are spiritual colors and are excellent for spirit communication. Pink is significant of love. White is purity and always is appropriate for any meditation. Yellow is for the intellect and green is for prosperity, growth, and healing. Whatever the meditation is for determines the color you should choose.

For the following meditations, you will be seeking to establish a meeting with a spirit teacher. Any of the following colors of candles would be appropriate: white, light blue, indigo, or purple. If you wish to use two candles, combine a white candle with any of the other colors.

It is always my suggestion to burn incense during meditations, unless you have severe allergies. Incense blesses the area in which you meditate and will carry your wishes to the gods—a belief of many. Select one of the following: jasmine, rose, patchouli, frankincense, sandalwood, or lilac.

Begin at your chosen time where no one will disturb you. Dress in loose-fitting clothing so nothing binds your body. Select a chair that is comfortable, but not too much so. You do not want to risk falling asleep. Some people prefer to sit on the floor, crossing their legs in a yogic fashion, with their backs against a wall for support. I don't recommend this position for a beginning meditator because energy needs to flow freely, and crossed legs inhibit the flow. This position is for the more experienced meditator, in my opinion. If you feel that you fall into the category of a more experienced meditator and have used the floor position effectively, then do so. However, if you are in the seated position, arrange your body so that your feet are flat on the floor. Whether seated or on the floor, place your hands in your lap with the palms up. This is a receptive pose and you will be able to feel the energy coming into the palms of your hands this way. Turn on the tape recorder and close your eyes to begin.

The Mountain

Inhale deeply through the nostrils and exhale slowly through slightly parted lips. *(Pause.)* Follow this action twice more, breathing deeply and slowly exhaling. *(Pause.)* Focus the attention to your feet. Stretch them out away from your body, then rotate your feet around, returning them to a comfortable position. *(Pause.)* Tense your feet and then tense your ankles. *(Pause.)* Release. Proceed in this manner of tensing the muscles all the way up your legs, tightening first the calves and then the thighs. *(Pause.)* Now release.

Tighten the buttocks and the stomach muscles. *(Pause.)* Release. Tense the entire arm area while also tightening the chest muscles. *(Pause.)* Now release. Pull the shoulders forward and then backward, holding each position for a few seconds and release. *(Pause.)* Rotate the shoulders several times forward and backward. *(Pause.)* Release. Bend the head slowly forward, backward, to each side, and back to center. *(Pause.)* Take two deep breaths through the nostrils and exhale between parted lips.

Visualize yourself standing at the foot of a grand mountain, your feet almost swallowed up in the green grass. Look up to the top of the mountain. See how high it is, reaching into the clouds. Observe the grandeur of the mountain and all of its details. *(Pause.)*

Now begin to climb the mountain. Don't be afraid. Spirit is assisting you. The climb will be an easy one, no matter how steep the incline. Your feet are light in weight, your body is limber, and your hands are strong. As you ascend the mountain, your feet feel as if they have wings attached. Your steps are so easy and sure, it would seem that your feet already know the path. Each rock is placed conveniently for your hands to grasp. It's almost like climbing a ladder, so fluid is your ascent. *(Pause.)*

Notice the tiny creatures that dart about between the rocks, observing your climb. They are harmless and you have no fear. *(Pause.)* Also notice the foliage that peaks out from between the cracks and crevices. *(Pause.)* As you look upward, you can see that the top of the mountain is nearing. *(Pause.)* Keep climbing. *(Pause.)* As you reach toward the next rock, the area begins to open somewhat. It is easier to stand more erect and the surface is not as jagged. Soon you are able to stand fully and walk on level ground. You are on top of the mountain. Look up. There is only sky above. A beautiful blue sky. Drink in the beauty. (*Pause.*) Observe the clouds above, so light and fluffy, appearing like frothy cream as they are poised overhead. (*Pause.*)

Notice ahead of you that the peak is not very broad and other mountains across the ravine can be seen. (*Pause.*) Walk across the peak to the other side so you can view the mountains across the way. (*Pause.*) A mammoth canyon falls beneath you, descending, it would seem, forever into the earth below. (*Pause.*) Majestic mountains rise up across from where you stand, with snowcaps jauntily decking the crown. (*Pause.*) Find a large rock to sit on and enjoy the view across the ravine. (*Pause longer.*)

Suddenly, you hear your name being called ever so softly. It is spirit calling. It is your spirit teacher. But where is the spirit? You realize the sound of the voice is coming from down in the ravine, below the cliff edge. Again you hear your name being called and this time the sound is closer. (*Pause.*) The spirit must be rising up alongside the mountain, you conclude. A third time the sound of your name greets your ears. (*Pause.*) Now the sound is so close, just a few feet away, but the spirit is not yet visible.

As the spirit ascends higher, you begin to see the top of the spirit's head rising just above the edge of the cliff.

(*Pause.*) With every second that ticks by, the head of the spirit becomes more visible as the spirit continues to rise above the cliff's edge. (*Pause.*) Your anticipation is growing. Your spirit teacher is so near. Now you can clearly see the top of the head, right down to the brow. (*Pause.*) With another few seconds passing, the eyes and nose are visible. (*Pause.*) Inhale one long, slow breath, and as you exhale slowly and deliberately, the full face comes into view. (*Pause.*)

The spirit floats easily upward now to allow you to see exactly what he or she is wearing. (*Pause.*) The spirit continues to rise, and at last you are able to see the entity clearly. (*Pause.*) Is the spirit feminine or masculine in appearance? (*Pause.*) Observe the color of the hair and eyes. (*Pause.*) Does he or she appear to be young, middle aged, or elderly? (*Pause.*) What clothing is being worn? (*Pause.*) What time in history do you believe this spirit represents? (*Pause.*)

Now ask the spirit to sit on a rock in front of you. (*Pause.*) As you sit facing your spirit teacher, ask, "What is your name?" (*Pause.*) "Where do you come from?" (*Pause.*) "What role do you play in my life?" (*Pause awhile.*) Ask any number of questions that you like of the spirit. (*Pause for a longer period.*)

When you are done, thank the spirit for coming. Express your gratitude for this wonderful encounter. Be sure to ask the spirit to meet you again at the same time. (*Pause.*)

When you wish to return to the here and now, take several deep breaths and begin to climb back down the mountain. (*Pause.*) It is such an easy journey. Your feet and hands seem to fly easily down the mountain path. (*Pause.*) Once back to the grassy area, take a deep breath (*pause*), wiggle your hands and feet (*pause*), and open your eyes when ready.

Now would be a good time to do a journal entry to record the experience. This will allow you to refer back to this first encounter at a later date to see how everything fits in with the big picture or has changed from this time.

The Beach

With your eyes closed and the body correctly positioned, inhale three times deeply, then forcefully exhale through the mouth. Allow the exhalation to be audible as you push the air out of your lungs. (*Pause.*) Visualize yourself at the top of a flight of rough, wooden, well-worn stairs, similar to what you would find descending from a boardwalk onto a sandy beach. (*Pause.*) Take a step down with your bare foot. Before you go to the next step, visualize the number ten. (*Pause.*)

As you continue to go down the steps, know that with each decreasing number, you will become more and more relaxed. As you visualize the number ten, take the next step and think "Relax." Relax. (*Pause.*) Breathe deeply. Visualize the number nine, take a step down and think "Relax." Relax. (*Pause.*) Breathe deeply. Number eight, step down, and relax. Relax. (*Pause.*) Breathe deeply. Visualize seven, step down, relax. Relax. (*Pause.*) Breathe deeply. And number six, step down, relax. Relax. (*Pause.*) Breathe deeply. Visualize five, step down, relax. Relax. (*Pause.*) Breathe deeply. Four, step down, relax. Relax. (*Pause.*) Breathe deeply. And three, step down, relax. Relax. (*Pause.*) Breathe deeply. Visualize two, step down, relax. Relax. (*Pause.*) Breathe deeply. And finally, number one, step to the bottom, and relax. Relax. (*Pause.*) Breathe deeply. You are completely relaxed now.

Now that you have arrived at the bottom of the stairs, you become aware that your bare feet are standing in sand. The sand is warm and gritty, forming soft pillows around your feet. Your toes sink into the soft sand. (*Pause.*) The ocean is thundering into the shoreline ahead, creating a roaring background to the sound of the seagulls flying overhead. Listen to the sounds of the beach. (*Pause.*) As the ocean rushes in with strength, white bubbles are left behind when the crystal water recedes back from whence it came. Watch how the water plays on the sand with its ebb and flow motion. (*Pause.*)

Feel the warmth under your feet as you walk across the sandy pillows to the wet, smooth sand along the shoreline. (*Pause.*) Creamy, textured sand squishes between your toes and oozes over the tops of your feet like pudding. (*Pause.*) Enjoy this sensual experience as you watch the waves build from the flat water surface far out in the ocean into the grand, forceful peaks of water that inevitably crash into the shore. (*Pause.*)

Begin to walk along the shoreline, heading north. (*Pause.*) Frequently, as you trek along, the ocean slaps into shore, swirling around your feet and rising upward, sometimes washing to your knees. (*Pause.*) Feel how cool and refreshing the water is as your feet and legs are bathed in the wet comfort of the ocean. Notice how tingly your skin feels because of the salt air puncturing your flesh and the summer sun basking you with its golden rays. (*Pause.*) You feel as if a special ray has enclosed you within a cylinder of protection, warming your spiritual nature and promising to reveal untold mysteries. (*Pause.*)

The sky is almost as blue as the ocean is aqua, not a cloud to be seen. (*Pause.*) The beach is empty, except for the sand crabs crawling nearby and seagulls hovering overhead, crowing down a greeting or two as they flap along with you. (*Pause.*)

As you continue walking along the shoreline, enjoying the surroundings, the faintest speck can be seen in the distance. At first it is just a dot. (*Pause.*) As you casually stroll along, the dot becomes bigger. (*Pause.*) You notice it is moving toward you at the same pace as you are approaching it. (*Pause.*) As this form draws closer, it is apparent it is a spiritual being. There is a beautiful aura surrounding the form, a special glow that appears to envelop this spirit. (*Pause.*) This is my spirit teacher, you think, as the entity continues the approach. (*Pause.*)

Now that the spirit has come much closer, it is easy to see the hair color and clothing. Take notice of all the colors present, hair, skin, clothing. (*Pause awhile.*) As the spirit draws still nearer, you are able to distinguish between the feminine or masculine of the spirit's appearance. (*Pause.*) You are easily able to discern the era the spirit represents in history. (*Pause.*) Observe the overall appearance and demeanor of your spirit teacher as he or she stands before you. (*Pause.*)

As you continue your journey up the coastline, the spirit turns, falls in step with you, and becomes your companion. (*Pause.*) Walk awhile with the spirit guide. Feel the presence beside you. (*Pause.*) Just ahead you notice that there are two benches, facing each other. Sit with your spirit teacher now and talk. It is the opportunity you have been waiting for. Communicate with your spirit guide. Ask the questions you desire to have answered. "What is your name?" (*Pause.*) "Where do you come from?" (*Pause.*) "What time in history did you live?" (*Pause longer.*) "What is your purpose with me?" (*Pause longer.*) "Do you have a message for me?" (*Pause longer.*) Ask your guide whatever other questions you wish. (*Pause longer.*)

When you feel that the time has come to close this session, bid the guide farewell and thank the spirit for coming. (*Pause.*) Walk back down the beach again, enjoying the ocean scene and the seagulls flying overhead. Begin to become focused on the here and now. (*Pause.*) Take several deep breaths. Wiggle your hands and feet. (*Pause.*) When you are ready, open your eyes.

The Castle

Begin by taking three deep, cleansing breaths. In (*pause*) and out. Repeat that action. In (*pause*) and out. Once again, in (*pause*) and out. Visualize a brilliant white light the size of a pinhead directly in front of you. (*Pause.*) This is God's white light of love and protection. Watch how it expands. (*Pause.*) And expands. (*Pause.*) And expands still further until it totally encloses you within. (*Pause.*) In your mind's eye, see the white light surrounding you on all sides. To the left. (*Pause.*) To the right. (*Pause.*) Behind you. (*Pause.*) In front. (*Pause.*) Overhead. (*Pause.*) And below. (*Pause.*)

Feel the comfort this white light energy brings. (*Pause.*) Bask in the white light energy of love. (*Pause.*) Feel this love permeate your body. Notice the prickles on your skin as it penetrates into your feet and ankles. (*Pause.*) Feel the tingle as the white light energy oozes into the pores of your legs. (*Pause.*)

Now, the loving light energy sinks gently into the trunk area of your body. Feel the warmth and comfort. (*Pause.*) Then the love energy glides into the pores of your arms and hands. Feel the tingle in the palms of your hands as the energy is absorbed. (*Pause.*) Now the white light energy enters into the neck, face, and head. (*Pause.*) As the white light energy fills your head, be aware of a lightness and floating feeling within. (*Pause.*) Your body and head are filled to almost bursting with white light energy. Every single cell of your body is saturated with the comforting energy of unconditional love. (*Pause.*) The intensity rises to such a degree, that this wonderful love energy begins to escape from the very top of your head. See and feel the energy as it leaves from your crown chakra, gushing upward in a mighty funnel. (*Pause.*) In your mind's eye, look upward through the tunnel of light. (*Pause.*) See how brilliant the light is as it curves around in a cylindrical fashion above. (*Pause.*)

Allow your body to float up into the funnel, gently traveling to a new place and time. (*Pause.*) Continue traveling through the bright white light tunnel of energy. (*Pause.*) As you rise out of the top of the funnel, you find yourself standing on a crystal pathway. It glistens and shines as you walk along the sidewalk made of crystal. You can even see your reflection gleaming back at you. (*Pause.*)

Up ahead you see a crystal palace. It is the most magnificent structure you have ever seen. (*Pause.*) Continue walking toward the crystal palace. (*Pause.*) Notice all the details of this glorious crystal structure as you walk. (*Pause.*) There are several glistening stairs leading to the front door. Begin to climb the stairs until you reach the top. (*Pause.*) Place your hand on the ornate door knob and swing open the door. (*Pause.*) Step inside. (*Pause.*) What do you see? (*Pause.*)

Begin to investigate the palace. Walk around. Touch the walls. (*Pause.*) Touch any of the articles present. Feel the texture of your surroundings. (*Pause.*) What sounds meet your ears? (*Pause.*) What aromas greet your nostrils? (*Pause.*)

Eventually you come to a hallway with a door at the end. (*Pause.*) Walk down the hallway toward the door. (*Pause.*) Continue walking as you observe the surroundings. Listen to the sounds and breathe the scents. (*Pause.*) When you come to the door, place your hand on the knob as you prepare to enter the room. (*Pause.*) Turn the knob and open the door. (*Pause.*) You discover that the room is empty, except for a flat white bench placed in the center of the room. (*Pause.*) Walk inside, toward the bench, and when you arrive there, sit down. (*Pause.*)

You instinctively know that your guide is in this room. You can feel the spiritual presence. (*Pause.*) Ask that your guide make its presence known. Sit for a moment as you attempt to feel the presence of your guide draw closer. (*Pause.*) You should feel the guide on either side of you or standing behind. (*Pause longer.*)

Now ask that the guide come forward slowly, in small increments, from wherever you feel the spirit is to stand in front of you. (*Pause.*) Ask the guide to step still closer until you can see a slight indication of one side in your peripheral vision. (*Pause.*) Again, ask that your guide come closer, until you are able to see more of the spirit's form. (*Pause.*) Continue this process until you are able to see the entire spirit standing before you. (*Pause longer.*)

What does the spirit look like? Is it a male or female figure? (*Pause.*) What color is the hair and how is it styled? (*Pause.*) What kind of clothes is the spirit wearing? (*Pause.*) What time in history do you believe the spirit is from? (*Pause.*) Observe anything else about the physical characteristics of your guide. (*Pause.*) Now, ask whatever questions you would like: "What is your name? (*Pause longer.*) "Where are you from?" (*Pause.*) "What is your purpose with me?" (*Pause longer.*) "Do you have a message for me?" (*Pause longer.*)

When you have concluded your meeting with your guide, bid the spirit farewell and thank the guide for coming. (*Pause.*) Arrange for another meeting the next day. (*Pause.*) When this is done, visualize yourself walking out of the room, down the hallway, and out the door of the crystal palace. (*Pause.*)

Walk down the stairs and back down the path until you return to the light tunnel. Slide back down the funnel gently. (*Pause.*) Take several deep breaths. (*Pause.*) Move your head from side to side. (*Pause.*) Shift your body around a little, and open your eyes when you are ready.

Once communication has been established, a simple meditation is all that is necessary in order to speak with your guides thereafter. Begin by choosing to meditate at your appropriate time, selecting a candle color, according to what you are attempting to accomplish, and your favorite incense, followed by soft music. Choose a technique to relax your mind and body, perhaps one of the methods outlined in the previous meditations. Then ask that the guide come forward. For instance: "Miko, are you there?" "Which one of my guides would like to speak with me today?" "Who is present? Please come forward so I may identify you." Then proceed to carry on a conversation as you would with any other living being.

If you are seeking a solution to a problem at work, for instance, ask for advice from the most appropriate guide for the situation. In your head ask, "Should I tell my boss that there is a conflict with a coworker?" Then sit in the silence, waiting for your answer. Listen to the silence intently. I like to think of it as turning your hearing on. The attention is focused on the ears and hearing; a vibration may even be felt. Also, be aware of images that float before your closed eyes. Notice any physical sensations you may feel. Certainly be conscious of any "feelings" regarding the work place that come over you at this time. Your spirit teachers will respond through clairvoyance, clairaudience, clairsentience, and/or clairgustance, whichever way that you have established communication. Don't be surprised if it takes awhile to receive at first. The communication will grow stronger each time you meditate and will be easier to establish. Clarity will eventually be what you experience.

As you progress, you will be able to ask for advice or assistance at any given time without having to sit down to meditate. Spirit can be helpful when you are sitting at your desk trying to find a solution to a computer glitch, or in a shopping mall while attempting to purchase the perfect birthday present for your partner. However, I would not encourage you to anticipate a guide manifesting in the middle of the aisle at Macy's department store to advise you! But you certainly could expect to receive an impression.

Many people have experienced what I like to affectionately call "random accosting" from relatives and friends who are in spirit. In other words, they receive unexpected visitations. Why not encourage a visit instead of longing for one, or being surprised as you walk down your dark hallway to the kitchen for a glass of milk at 3 A.M.?

I would suggest using a similar process to communicate with a loved one as you would to contact a spirit guide. Light a pink or white candle, burn your favorite incense, and play soft music at your appropriate time for meditation. I also like to place a photograph of the relative or friend next to the candle when I am meditating for the purpose of receiving communication from spirits of my loved ones who have passed on. A photographic image contains the energy of that person, so it helps to encourage the visitation. When everything is in place and you have used a technique to relax, invite your relative or friend to join you. Beckon them as you would normally. "Grandma, I would love for you to come talk with me." "I miss you, Mama, please come visit me now." "Charlie, I am here. Come to me now." Ask what you will of them, be it advice, comfort, questions about themselves, whatever you desire.

As with all communication attempts, I cannot guarantee that this particular method or any other will work to enable you to speak with your wife, brother, uncle, grandmother, or best friend since college. I wish I could make that guarantee, but if I were to make such a claim, it would be false. For hundreds of reasons they may be occupied or simply not wish to communicate, which probably has nothing to do with you personally. Remember, spirit also has freedom of choice, and their perception from the other side is different than when they were on the earth plane. Although they still carry their own unique characteristics, they have "seen the light," and through their new vision they perceive earth life differently. Our loved ones are still there to help us from the other side, but they are not our devoted slaves, willing to come at our whim. As with spirit teachers, we do not want to become overly dependent on our loved ones in spirit. We have to respect their new life and recognize that they will be present with us when it is appropriate for them and us. If an attempt to communicate with a loved one does not work out, simply try again at another time.

Also, it is important to mention that after a recent passing, you do not want to cause a spirit to be earthbound with your grieving attempts to communicate. It would be unhealthy for you emotionally to keep one of your relatives or friends earthbound, and certainly not in the best interests of the spirit that is trying to live and evolve in his or her new world.

Spontaneous appearances in spirit from recently deceased people are a common occurrence during the early stages of a passing. But a time will come when you must let go and release the spirit so he or she may go to the light. I would feel after two weeks maximum, if you are still holding onto your loved one's spirit energy, it is truly time to set him or her free. After a fashion, the spirit will be back to visit when the time is correct for them. It is at that point when a communication attempt is appropriate for all parties concerned.

You will find communicating with spirit an interesting process and surely to be very rewarding on both the mundane and spiritual levels. I wish you much love and happiness in your awareness of your spirit companions. May this be a blessed union of hearts and spirits, and may you always know that you are loved and protected by spirit.

The end is just the beginning.

APPENDIX ONE

Sylvia DeLong speaks with high regard about a domestic helper guide who came to her cooking aid (see chapter 5). Sylvia never cooked until after her mother had to go into a nursing home. Mary, a sweet Scottish woman, came to her rescue, impressing her with recipes that Sylvia herself would never have been able to create without the assistance of this spirit lady. Sylvia shared one of those recipes with me and now I'd like to share it with you.

Scottish Stew

3	potatoes, cut up
2–3	carrots, diced
3	onions, diced
3	stalks of celery, diced
½–1	lb. lean stew beef
	Kitchen Bouquet

Cut the beef into small chunks and brown. Dip the meat in flour first and cook in olive oil in an iron skillet. Put everything in a 2-quart covered dish, but no water, just two teaspoons of Kitchen Bouquet (flavoring). Add salt and pepper to taste or any other spices you might like. Bake in the oven at 350 degrees for 1–1½ hours, or until tender.

I tried this recipe twice. My suggestions would be that if you use a full pound of meat, a larger cooking container is necessary. I also added about a ¼ cup of water the second time, and that made a big difference. The meat was tender, moist, and delicious, without a lot of liquid after cooking.

GLOSSARY

Astral projection or travel: This is an action where the spirit leaves the body during a sleep state or through a conscious effort, and travels into a spiritual dimension or an area on the earth plane different from where the physical body is located.

Cabinet: This is an enclosure within a room, sometimes portable, usually with a curtain drawn across the entrance, in which a medium goes into a trance state while seated. The confinement of the medium's energy within the cabinet aids her or him to build up energy for the purpose of producing phenomena.

Chakra: This is a Sanskrit word meaning "something that rotates." Chakras are seven conically shaped rays of energy, with the main energy centers located along the body's vertical axis. They are the root, which is at the base of the spine; the sacral, two inches below the belly button; the solar plexus, in the waist area; the heart;

throat; third eye, which is slightly above the eyebrows in the center of the forehead; and crown, the very top of the head.

Circle: To sit in circle is a term used to describe an action where people gather regularly to meditate for the purpose of contacting spirits, usually in someone's home. There may or may not be a teacher present.

Development class: This is a class where a person may learn to enhance his or her psychic and mediumistic abilities under the tutelage of an experienced teacher who is a psychic or medium.

Ectoplasm: This is a Greek word meaning "exteriorized substance." This cloudy substance streams out of mediums when they are demonstrating phenomena, usually from the mouth or nose, and frequently from the solar plexus, but can emanate from any orifice. Generally, it forms around the spirit to give the entity a visible shape when a spirit is manifesting during a séance to afford the participants the opportunity to see a spirit. Ectoplasm may also surround a spirit when the entity manifests in daily life, outside of a séance setting.

Going to the light: This is a term used to describe when a person ceases to live in the physical plane and his or her spirit is making the transition into the spirit side of life. A brilliant white light has been reported being seen, according to people who have had near-death experiences, when a person is dying and entering the spirit world. It also has connotations of a higher spiritual presence, such as God.

Karma: This could be referred to as lessons in life. Some religions and many people believe our souls come to the earth to work through specific issues, or karma, so that we may grow spiritually.

Kundalini: This is a storehouse of vital energy, or creative life force, located at the base of the spine, symbolized as a coiled snake. It is the serpent of life, fire, and wisdom. When this power of the spirit is awakened, it opens the chakras and can produce psychic powers.

Manifest: This is the appearance of a spirit through numerous means, such as a visible form, by sound, or touch.

Materialization: A materialization is when a spirit appears either during a séance or chooses to manifest in front of someone under ordinary circumstances.

Medium: A medium is a person who is sensitive to the vibrations from the spirit world. He or she is able to communicate with those on the spirit side of life through various means, delivering information and assistance to those who ask. All mediums are also psychics.

Messages: Messages can be greetings, information, warnings, comfort, and advice that one might receive through the mediumship of an individual from a spirit. Usually these messages are brief and delivered to a group of people individually for the purpose of demonstrating the continuity of life. Spiritualists conduct message services as part of their religious services.

Mini-reading: This is an activity where a person sits for a reading with a medium for a short period of time, such as fifteen minutes, at a reduced fee. Frequently many mediums will offer this service to the public as a fundraiser for the church.

Natural law: These are principles that are operating in nature that include what is innate within us and throughout all life, forming the orderly condition of things in nature. The understanding of these principles can often determine our actions and/or the consequences of our actions. In other words, we can create our own happiness or unhappiness by the choices we make.

Nature spirits: Nature spirits are spiritual beings, frequently invisible to the human eye, titled fairies, gnomes, salamanders, etc., who are involved with nature. They are also referred to as spirits of water, air, fire, and earth.

Other side of life or other side: This is the spirit world where one goes after passing away.

Physical phenomena: This is used as a means to demonstrate the continuity of life. Some examples would be the materialization of a spirit from a cabinet, a trumpet rising, a table moving, or voices emanating from a person or object.

Platform: A stage used by mediums for the purpose of delivering messages or lectures.

Psychic: A knowing, sensing ability. This is a mental act, such as knowing who is calling on the telephone before answering, or sensing from a distance that your children are in danger. Everyone is psychic to a certain degree. All professional psychics are not necessarily mediums.

Reader: A reader is someone who gives mediumistic or psychic readings or counseling, often referred to as a medium or spiritual counselor.

Reading: This is an activity where a person visits a medium or psychic for the purpose of receiving information/assistance regarding his or her life. This term could also apply to someone who would offer tarot card services. Not all means of receiving a reading necessarily offer communication with spirit, as would that received from a medium.

Séance: This term was popular in the 1880s and early 1900s when people would gather in a darkened room to contact spirits through various means. A more accurate definition currently would be when people sit in classes for development purposes. Technically, when one sits in a circle during classes, they are participating in a séance.

Silver cord: The silver cord is an ethereal conduit or "pipeline" through which the energy or soul life flows to the physical body. It is like the umbilical cord that goes from a mother to her baby, providing the child a soul gateway and physical energy line from the mother. (See Ecc. 12: 6–7.) In full-form materializations, it is what bonds the spirit to the medium, thereby providing energy to the spirit.

Skotograph: This is a phenomena used to demonstrate the continuity of life by using photographic paper during meditation and placing it in solutions for development. Spirit faces appear when the film has developed.

Spirit: This is a word that has several meanings. Spirit can be defined as a luminous, ethereal form, once human that now is deceased, and living in another plane of existence. It is also a term used for God or to denote a higher spiritual power.

Spiritualism: Spiritualism is a religion, science, and philosophy that believes in continuous life, based upon communication with those who live in the spirit world, as demonstrated through mediumship. Through such communication one is able to receive guidance in mundane and spiritual matters from spiritual beings who are knowledgeable. They embrace personal responsibility and the belief that the doorway to reformation is never closed. Like all other positive religions, Spiritualism also teaches that we should follow the Golden Rule.

Spiritualist: This is a person who believes, as the basis of his or her religion, in the continuity of life and personal responsibility, and endeavors to mold his or her character and conduct in accordance with the highest teaching derived from communion with the spirit world. He or she may or may not be a medium.

Symbol: This is where an interpretation can be deciphered from seeing an object depicted during meditation or in a dream state.

Synchronicity: Events that happen, appearing to be coincidental, as in simultaneous events.

Third eye: This is one of the energy centers each person possesses, also referred to as a chakra. It is located between the eyes and slightly above the eyebrows. It is sometimes referred to as the all-seeing eye.

Trumpet: An instrument used to demonstrate physical phenomena. It is usually made of lightweight aluminum, cone-shaped, and collapses into itself for storage.

Unfoldment: The hoped-for end result of sitting in circles or classes for the purpose of learning to communicate with the spirit world and, eventually, "unfold" mediumistic abilities.

White light: This is representative of God or a higher spiritual power, filled with love and protection from all harm.

SUGGESTED READING

Andrews, Ted. *Enchantment of the Faerie Realm*. St. Paul, Minn.: Llewellyn Worldwide, 1993.

Bethards, Betty. *The Dream Book: Symbols for Self-Understanding*. New York, N.Y.: Harper Collins, 1997.

Todeschi, Keven. *Encyclopedia of Symbolism*. New York, N.Y.: Perigee Books, 1996.

White Eagle. *Spiritual Unfoldment 2*. Marina Del Rey, Calif.: DeVorss & Company, 2000.

INDEX

A

American Indian (see *Native American*)

angels, 47, 49–50, 68, 92–93, 118

astral projection/travel, 95

Aubrey, Patti, 6, 24–25, 44, 92–93

aura, 20, 86, 102–105, 170

automatic drawing, 128, 130

automatic writing, 126–127

Avon on Gorge, 16

B

Bluebell, 109

Buddha, 67, 73

bullroar, 94

Burroughs, H. Gordon, 28

C

cabinet, 106–107, 109

Callin, Ruth, 19–20, 96, 99–100

Camp Silverbell, 109

Cassadaga, xiv, 27, 37, 40, 48, 60, 75, 80, 89–90, 92–93, 95, 97, 100, 111, 118, 123

chemist guide, 54–55

Cholula, 15–16

clairaudience, 23, 32, 175

clairgustance, 28, 32, 175

clairsentience, 25–27, 32, 175

clairvoyance, 21–23, 32, 131, 175

Cleopatra, 72

coincidence, 29–30, 155

creator guide, 64, 66

Custance, Kenneth, 92

D

Davis, Diane, 2, 9, 30, 59, 82, 127

DeLong, Hilda, 16–17, 53–54, 66, 80, 109–110

DeLong, Leland, 12, 17–18, 24, 109–110

DeLong, Sylvia, xiv, 9, 12, 15–18, 20, 23–24, 51–54, 59, 66–67, 78, 80, 109–110, 123–124, 131, 137, 141, 147, 149

detach, 151–152

doctor guide, 44, 46–47, 50–54, 57, 69, 116

domestic helpers, 66

doorkeeper (see *gatekeeper guide*)

E

Eckroad, Bertha, 108

ectoplasm, 54, 87, 107

Ellison, Fran, 77

Elvis, 72

energy, 2, 12, 20, 27, 48, 63, 76, 81–83, 103, 118, 124–126, 132–138, 163, 171–172, 176, 178

etherealizations, 108

F

fairies, 68

Ford, Arthur, 106

Franklin, Ben, 72

Frederich, Jerry, 13, 78–79, 93–95, 112–113, 139–140, 160

G

gatekeeper guide, 10, 13, 45–46, 68–69

Gates, Louis, 13, 21, 40, 52, 151

Gates, Marie, 47–52

guardian angels, 49–50, 68

H

Hammond, Billy, 80

healing, 4, 46–47, 49–52, 54, 73, 162

Hermann, Steve, 27, 89

Hoover, Warren, 2, 27–28, 55, 71, 75, 82, 106–109, 122, 127, 144

Houdini, 106

I
inspirational writing,
126–127

J
Jackson, Rev., 63
Jefts, Lena, 106
Jesus, 3, 67, 72–73, 92
joy guide, 61

K
Kirlian photography,
101–105
Kola, 16
Krishna, 67, 73
kundalini, 103

L
life guide, 45–46
Lilla, Marie, xv–xvi, 20,
37–38, 62, 91, 111, 123,
156

M
manifestation, 4, 67, 74,
92–93
master teacher, 21, 45, 58,
62–64, 69, 72
materialization, 54,
106–109
meditation, xvi, 11, 13, 15,
21, 25, 54, 57–58, 65,
67, 69–72, 76, 79–80,
88, 90, 96–97, 108, 114,
124, 127–130, 140–144,
147, 153–156, 159–162,
174, 176
medium, xiv, xvi, 1, 5, 9,
19, 22, 25, 27–28,
39–40, 46, 48, 54, 58,
75, 80, 88–89, 91–92,
95–97, 99, 106–107,
109, 114, 118, 124,
149–152, 154
Miko, 63, 175
Myers, Alice, 100
Myers, Arthur, 100–101,
106

N
Napoleon, 72
Native American, 33, 44,
58–59, 145
native guide (see also
Native American), 33,
44, 58–59, 69, 131, 145

O
orbs, 118
Ouija board, 38, 121–124

P
Page, Eloise, 40–41, 75, 92,
104, 155
Parrish, Ethel Post,
106–108

past lives, 14–15
philosopher guide, 57–58
protector, 2, 45, 59, 110
psychic, 1, 3, 59, 86, 91, 101, 106, 130
psychic artist, xiv, 1
Pyramids of Cholula, 16

R
Reese, Johnny, 109
Relda, Catherine, 114

S
St. Germain, 67, 73
Schmitt, June, 75
séance, 28, 106, 109, 132, 138
Sikora, Arlene, 2, 20–21, 86–88, 101–105, 113–114, 122, 128–129, 144–147, 150–151
Silverbell, 106–107, 109
Skotograph, 112–114
Sophia, 67
spirit, xiii–xvi, 1–7, 9–33, 35–40, 43–61, 64–83, 85–87, 89–90, 92, 95–97, 99–100, 106–110, 112, 117–119, 121–129, 131–132, 134–141, 144–153, 155–157, 159–162, 164–166, 170, 173–178

spirit guide, 3, 14, 17, 37, 40, 45, 47–48, 56–57, 68, 72, 156, 160, 170, 176
spirit teacher, 17, 27, 45, 71, 106–107, 109, 159, 161–162, 165–166, 170
Spiritualist, xiv, xvi, 1, 3, 28, 39, 73, 86, 88–89, 95, 106, 142
Symbols, 21–22, 31, 152–155
synchronicity, 29–31, 64

T
table tipping, 131–135, 137–138
teacher guide, 41, 56, 58
Toltec Indian, 15–16, 110
trumpet séance, 108–109

U
universal master, 55, 67, 73, 75

V
Virgin Mary, 74–75

W
Weigl, Lillian, 13, 20, 28, 50, 60, 69–70, 73, 78, 85–86, 99–101

REACH FOR THE MOON

Llewellyn publishes hundreds of books on your favorite subjects! To get these exciting books, including the ones on the following pages, check your local bookstore or order them directly from Llewellyn.

Order by Phone
- Call toll-free within the U.S. and Canada, 1-877-NEW WRLD
- In Minnesota, call (651) 291-1970
- We accept VISA, MasterCard, and American Express

Order by Mail
- Send the full price of your order (MN residents add 7% sales tax) in U.S. funds, plus postage & handling to:
  Llewellyn Worldwide
  P.O. Box 64383, Dept. 1-56718-530-4
  St. Paul, MN 55164-0383, U.S.A.

Postage & Handling
- **Standard** (U.S., Mexico, & Canada)

If your order is:

$20.00 or under, add $5.00

$20.01–$100.00, add $6.00

Over $100, shipping is free

(Continental U.S. orders ship UPS. AK, HI, PR, & P.O. Boxes ship USPS 1st class. Mex. & Can. ship PMB.)

- **Second Day Air** (Continental U.S. only): $10.00 for one book + $1.00 per each additional book
- **Express** (AK, HI, & PR only) [Not available for P.O. Box delivery. For street address delivery only.]: $15.00 for one book + $1.00 per each additional book
- **International Surface Mail:** Add $1.00 per item
- **International Airmail:** Books—Add the retail price of each item; Non-book items—Add $5.00 per item

Please allow 4–6 weeks for delivery on all orders.
Postage and handling rates subject to change.

Discounts
We offer a 20% discount to group leaders or agents. You must order a minimum of 5 copies of the same book to get our special quantity price.

Free Catalog
Get a free copy of our color catalog, *New Worlds of Mind and Spirit*. Subscribe for just $10.00 in the United States and Canada ($30.00 overseas, airmail). Call 1-877-NEW WRLD today!

Visit our website at www.llewellyn.com for more information.

Women Celebrating Life

A Guide to Growth & Transformation

ELIZABETH OWENS

Whether you're turning 21 or 50, having a baby or entering menopause, you can embrace and honor the events in your life through meaningful rituals. In solitude, you can perform ceremonies that will release pent-up emotions, soothe old wounds, and nurture the feminine spirit.

This book is a how-to manual written to help women manifest a more fulfilling existence. It gives specifics on how to perform ceremonies to raise a woman's consciousness, attract happy circumstances, and promote healing of the emotions. In an age where society sings the praises of the young, *Women Celebrating Life* recognizes and cheers the spiritual attributes of women who have experienced life.

1-56718-508-8
216 pp., 7½ x 9⅛ $12.95

Contact the Other Side

7 Methods for Afterlife Communication

KONSTANTINOS

Are you ready to make contact with loved ones on the other side? One of the nation's foremost vampire experts now turns his talents to the age-old quest for communication with the dead. This is the first book in the modern marketplace to focus on practical, usable techniques for communicating with spirits.

Whether you've been frustrated in the past by afterlife books that cite case studies but no usable methods, or are just now entering the world of paranormal communication, your search for proof is over. You don't have to be an electronics whiz or master of a secret occult discipline to capture the voices and images of the dead on audio and video tape, or to communicate with them via your mind alone.

This book will guide you to the most awe-inspiring experiences you'll ever have while still alive—to your own contact with deceased loved ones and other souls.

Speak with them. They're waiting.

1-56718-377-8
240 pp., 6 x 9, bibliog, index $14.95

Destiny of Souls
New Case Studies of Life Between Lives

MICHAEL NEWTON, PH.D.

A pioneer in uncovering the secrets of life, internationally recognized spiritual hypnotherapist Dr. Michael Newton takes you once again into the heart of the spirit world. His groundbreaking research was first published in the best-selling *Journey of Souls*, the definitive study on the afterlife. Now, in *Destiny of Souls*, the saga continues with seventy case histories of real people who were regressed into their lives between lives. Dr. Newton answers the requests of the thousands of readers of the first book who wanted more details about various aspects of life on the other side.

Hear the stories of people in deep hypnosis:
- Why we are on earth
- Spiritual settings where souls go after death
- Ways spirits connect with and comfort the living
- Spirit guides and the council of wise beings who interview us after each life
- Who is a soulmate and linkages between soul groups and human families
- Soul recreation and travel between lives

Also available in Spanish.

1-56718-499-5
6 x 9, 384 pp., illus.   **$14.95**

Messages and Miracles
Extraordinary Experiences of the Bereaved

LOUIS E. LAGRAND, PH.D.

In this moving and compassionate work, one of the pioneers in after-death communication (ADC) research explores the reasons why ADCs occur and how they help the bereaved.

Based on his counseling experience, interviews with numerous people who have had contact with a deceased loved one, and the many questions people have asked him since the the release of his first book, *After Death Communication*, LaGrand unfolds an untapped source of support for the bereaved and those who attempt to comfort them.

Learn whether contact experience is simply the stress of bereavement or an authentic communication, how it can help you establish a new relationship with the deceased, and how to talk to children who report the experience. Read actual accounts of ADCs which have never before appeared in print. *Also available in Spanish.*

1-56718-406-5
336 pp., 6 x 9, illus.   **$12.95**